TELL ME
ABOUT THE
HOLY
SPIRIT

"and About Revival"

DEAN BATES

INK START MEDIA
5710 W Gate City Blvd Ste K #284
Greensboro, NC 27407

READERS COMMENTS

CORDEEL'S COMMENTS:

This, Dean's book on the Holy Spirit is a must read for all those who want to get to know the living, Holy Spirit more and how to obtain more of His Power for their life. It's also for those of us who want a deeper, richer, and more fulfilling experience with the Holy Spirit. Dean's passion to pass along these facts about and experiences with the Holy Spirit is truly life changing for seekers and believers alike! This book opens up the amazing answers to questions on who the Holy Spirit is, what He does for us, His sense of humor, His awesome and amazing wisdom and so much more.

Dean - thank you for being obedient to God's direction and sticking to the gigantic task of completing this book. Even with countless obstacles, you never wavered! You kept saying its God's project and He will make a way, and He certainly did. And . . . I learned a lot from that amazing faith that you often verbalized to me! This book will change countless lives as the Lord will direct. My prayer is that the book will do for others what it has done for me, and draw many closer to the Lord and to His Holy Spirit.

—Cordel Batchelor, Esq

HANS' COMMENTS:

This dark world desperately needs this book, "Tell Me about the Holy Spirit!" In my many years of studying scripture and seeking the Spirit's wisdom, I have never experienced such a clear description and inspirational presentation of the Holy Spirit. In addition, the personal testimonies really help bring the Spirit to real life! This book needs to go far and wide, to all corners of the world!

—**Hans Brouwer**

JENNIFER'S COMMENTS:

Christians throughout the world are familiar with reciting prayers, singing psalms, reading from the Bible and listening to sermons that very often mention the Holy Spirit. However, who the Holy Spirit is and what He is all about may be a mystery to many who are in a personal journey. Spoken from the heart, this author through his own words and numerous testimonies of his and others passionately explains the power of the Holy Spirit and the role He can play in our lives if we only let him in. Full of scriptural references and religious songs, "Tell Me about the Holy Spirit" is a thought-provoking, eye-opening, enlightening must-read for all Christians regardless of how well you think you understand the Holy Spirit. This highly recommended life-changing book should be placed on the top of everyone's reading list.

—**Jennifer Bates McMahon**

DEBBY'S COMMENTS:

His book about the Holy Spirit is something that everyone seeking a better life needs to read. Not enough has been preached or talked about in clarity for the common worshiper to realize that the Spirit is alive 24/7 in all believers! We find examples throughout this book of friends as well as the author of real-life experiences of guidance, protection, and encouragement from the Holy Spirit. This book is a must-read for deniers, doubters and believers alike!

—**Debby Brouwer**

SONJA'S COMMENTS:

As a dear friend of Dean's throughout the several years that it took him to compose this book, I have come to appreciate the deep passion and clear calling that He has for helping others find a better life available from the spiritual help available to all who would just believe it. This inspired writing is amazingly easy to read and understand. Dean writes from the heart, attributing inspiration that comes to him from the Holy Spirit as he was composing this book.

—**Sonja Weaver**

TABLE OF CONTENTS

CHAPTER 1

TO BEGIN WITH 1

CHAPTER 2

IS GOD REAL? 7

CHAPTER 3

WHO IS JESUS? 13

CHAPTER 4

INTRODUCTION TO THE HOLY SPIRIT 17

CHAPTER 5

WHAT IS A CHRISTIAN REVIVAL? 23

CHAPTER 6

THE HOLY SPIRIT IN OUR DAILY LIFE 25

CHAPTER 7

WHAT THE BIBLE SAYS ABOUT THE HOLY SPIRIT 29

CHAPTER 8

HOW THE HOLY SPIRIT GETS INVOLVED 35

CHAPTER 9

EXPERIENCING THE HOLY SPIRIT IN CAR ISSUES 41

CHAPTER 10

THE EFFECTS OF THE HOLY SPIRIT IN US 45

CHAPTER 11

THEIR INCREDIBLE SPIRIT 51

CHAPTER 12

    MY BROTHER NEIL...55

CHAPTER 13

    KAREN'S WALK WITH THE HOLY SPIRIT 57

CHAPTER 14

    MORE OF KAREN'S WALK WITH THE HOLY SPIRIT 63

CHAPTER 15

    TRIP TO SOUTH CAROLINA 67

CHAPTER 16

    PASTOR JIMMIE'S TESTIMONY..71

CHAPTER 17

    A CATHOLIC GIRL AND THE HOLY SPIRIT.......................77

CHAPTER 18

    MY LAZARUS MOMENT...83

CHAPTER 19

    LORRAINE'S TESTIMONY...91

CHAPTER 20

    CORDEL'S TESTIMONY..97

CHAPTER 21

    A MOVIE OF YOUR LIFE...113

CHAPTER 22

    CONCLUDING THOUGHTS TO PONDER........................117

CHAPTER 23

    PROCLAMATION..121

CHAPTER 1
TO BEGIN WITH

"All scripture references are to the New International Version (NIV) of the Bible".

Since we all are coming from totally different backgrounds, we need to start with some common understandings of God. Related to God is the Trinity – the three in one – God the Father, the Son Jesus, and the Holy Spirit. Thus Chapter 2.

The reality of Jesus' ministry is without question historically, but His power in our life is a spiritual matter that involves the unseen world. It poses a question that each of us must resolve individually, no one can do it for us: "Does Jesus know me personally with a power over my life?". When I was faced with a serious problem in my life that I was sharing with a friend, he asked me if I had invited Jesus into my life? My reply was "I am an engineer – if I don't understand it, how can I believe it?" My friend's reply was, "You are asking to know the power of God. You have to accept it in faith as it is the unseen world." He never imposes Himself and, therefore, everyone must invite Him into your heart and believe in His crucifixion and resurrection. The purpose of Chapter 3 is to help the reader with this critical decision.

And now in Chapter 4 I address the involvement by the Trinity in the everyday issues of life. This is where the Holy Spirit comes in, the living Spirit that is in all believers 24/7, that knows all our past in detail, our present issues, and has a plan for our future if we are willing to let Him into our life. This is discussed in Chapter 5. Relevant directly to the Holy Spirit is what our society is currently experiencing - what is referred to as a "Revival" or "A Great Awakening." This is discussed in Chapter 6.

I then get into the details of life with the Holy Spirit beginning with my testimonies and then others who have experienced the wonder of the Holy Spirit active in a specific event.

But even before that, I want to address a dilemma that I have been dealing with all my spiritual life, as I was confronted with it again now while developing this book. The issue is – what are my sins that need to be confessed? Not that I consider myself to be sinless in the sight of God, but what does He see in me that needs to be addressed?

I grew up in a devoted, nurturing Christian family with loving and caring parents, grandparents, aunts and uncles that loved the Lord. We faithfully attended church with an abundance of fellowship and with many friends also having strong faiths. When I think of humble, I think of all those who had a part to play in my growing years, with their tender, loving spirits. I loved going to church, participating in Vacation Bible School in our church for one week and then in another church for another week. I was committed to never missing the weekly Sunday School class, and I collected many certificates for each year of faithful attendance. I enjoyed being in the choir, youth group, and youth retreats. I became a pianist and played piano/organ duets with the church organist. I have always wanted to do only the right thing, was a compliant son, and never wanted to do anything to bring embarrassment to my family and teachers in school.

During my adult life, I graduated from West Point that has the very strong honor code to live by. I have always been committed to honesty, integrity, reliability in all ways and being faithful to my Lord. Therefore, whenever I have been confronted by scripture to confess my sins, what do I have to confess? I'm sure that I am not sinless, but what are they and once known I will correct them? When an International Day of Prayer for our country occurred recently, we were all confronted with the Lord saying in 2 Chronicles 7:14, that "God would heal our land *if we would humble ourselves, pray, seek Him and turn from our wicked ways*". This scripture presented me with issues to deal with that has provoked the following understandings as I pondered these concerns while developing this book.

1. To be humble for the Lord does not mean necessarily just gentle and kind to each other. In the Lord's world it means to get on your knees in humbleness and sincerity to the Lord! You may say, "But I don't feel comfortable doing that – I never have." Consider for a moment the response that God might say in reply to that – "Are you too proud – is that too commonplace?"

2. When it comes to prayer, it is not just to meet your specific needs and desires, it is for Him to invoke His power and will for us individually for others as well as you. But first, it should be in sincere gratitude to Him for all the great things He has already done. Lifting up our concerns for this country and the world needs to have the total faith and trust that He is still in complete control over every detail of the world, past, present and all circumstances of our future, all of the deeds, actions and attitudes that are not conforming to His will. It is readily apparent that satan is having a hay-day with this world today, but all of his actions are known by our God, and He has a plan to ultimately address them. Prayer is not a continual reminder to the Lord of our needs – He already knows them. When lifted them up to Him, He does not need a continual reminder. He never forgets our prayer needs but answers them in His way and in His time as it fits into the plan that He has for us individually. After being lifted up to Him, our prayer concern needs to be turned into a praise to Him that He knows the need and takes on the obligation to meet them in His time and in His way.

3. To seek His face means to spend quality time, uninterrupted, devoted to not only lifting up our concerns, but more importantly to develop a *personal relationship* with Him. He has created us – each of us uniquely- for the primary purpose of us developing our individual relationship with Him as our Shepherd. We are little more than sheep, not knowing where we are going day by day, needing to be

protected, provided for, and guided through the minefields of our life.

4. It is a sin to be ungrateful, for all good things come from Him. Do we really believe that from God's perspective, the United States is at the *very top of all the countries in the world* that have received His blessings? Our founding fathers dedicated this country to Him and, although we have struggled to live according to His ways, He has been faithful to us with the freedoms and quality of life that is the envy of the world. How can we thank Him enough that we were not born in poverty or having lived under an oppressive regime?

5. Do you really appreciate the freedoms that we have and thank Him for his blessings, for inspiring our founding fathers, and especially be thankful for all

6. those who have given their lives in defense of this country? Think of the millions of people that have lost their lives in defense of the freedoms that we enjoy. Think of the billions of people in the world that have lost their lives in their quest for the freedoms that we take for granted.

7. Do you really realize how far our spiritual enthusiasm and moral values have eroded through the years? The quality of life that we had during the great depression when I was born in the 1930's has now been *degraded in every way* and, at the same time, our prosperity has significantly increased. How is it possible that the more blessing we have received, the less appreciative we are to the One where all good things come from?

8. Do we really appreciate the blessing of having a Bible in our home? Millions of Christians in the world would love to have one and we often have many copies, of different versions, that are often never used. In the early pioneer days of this country, many did not have textbooks for their schools, and the Bible was used to learn to read, spell, expand our vocabulary, and to study scripture. And now Bibles are restricted as well as prayer.

9. Do we really consider the fact that we have the very best medical care in the world, one that is aggressively promoting vaccines to counter the latest virus that is significantly affecting the entire world? In addition, the internet is readily available to help research many all-natural therapies and comments from knowledgeable healthcare professionals that can address the health concerns that we are experiencing.

10. Do you seriously treat your body as a "temple of the Holy Spirit", that is living in you 24/7? Do you feed it the right foods, control your weight, exercise as you know that you should? Do you abuse it with substances such as drugs, smoking and alcohol? Are you aware that your body needs the exercise that comes from the work that we now avoid with power-everything's?

11. Is your first priority to use your income to commit the first 10% to the church? Or is it to your retirement plan, paying for a new car or other obligations to make your life more comfortable and secure from having to depend on the Lord for providing your needs in the future? If you are tithing your income, what are you doing with the excess – paying for continuing accumulation of creature comforts for yourself, or are you helping provide for the needs of the less fortunate? Think of the people in this great country that right now have lost everything from hurricanes, floods, wildfires, the virus, and even violence. Is your daily search for a spiritual relationship limited to the daily devotional along with a quick prayer for your needs? Are you *truly, in earnest, seeking a relationship with the Lord?* The true desire of the Lord is for you to realize that He has given you, as a believer, the gift of the Holy Spirit that He wants you to realize is with you every moment of every day.

12. In your employment or with whatever you are doing in life, do you *fully believe that you are working for the Lord?* Do you appreciate that, if you have the Lord in your life, the success that you have experienced is a blessing from the Lord? Or the that He is fully aware of the struggles that you are going through has the Lord in it with total awareness of all the details, and that He has a better plan than you could ever conceive? Are you focused on having or needing a job that provides benefits, with the very highest income, in order to retire without financial needs for the rest of your life – so that you won't need Him? Or are you seeking the employment that the Lord directs for you in order to advance your relationship with Him, fully aware that He will provide for all your needs in the future? He knows your future in every detail, and you don't. Seriously consider that He has a better plan for your future than you could ever devise!

13. Do you sincerely treat the Bible as a living document, providing you the very best advice for how to live your life, in every detail? Do you understand that in your daily search for what the Lord wants for you, His primary method of communicating His desires for you are through the Bible in daily devotions, personal study, and personal prayer and meditation? We must always remember that He cannot get through to us in response to our prayers and appeals to Him unless we also take time for Him to respond. Time alone with Him, including quiet meditation, is critical as otherwise He can not get through to us.

14. How do you stack up with your compliance with the 10 Commandments? As an example:

    a. You shall have no other gods before me – do you spend more time with money matters than in daily quality time devoted to Him in praise and thanksgiving?

    b. Do you ever misuse the name of the Lord, for He promises to everyone that does so, He will hold guilty?

c. Remember the sabbath day and keep it Holy. What do you do on Sunday – the Lord declared it a day of rest? Do you consider it as such or are you going on without considering this a "commandment" for your life?

d. Honor your father and mother. How do you and your children stack up? Does the younger generation consider the internet the answer to all questions in life or, do you and they appreciate that wisdom comes with age, and knowledge is not a substitute for wise counsel?

e. You shall not commit adultery. This is a major issue that is addressed in the Bible in many places with serious consequences. What is your stand on this when it comes to your life, and also with tolerating your children's attitude towards this Commandment?

f. You shall not covet your neighbor's belongings. Why buy a new car when the old one is still reliable? Why "update" your home when the old is still functional? Why devote significant spare time to entertainment, playing or participating in games, etc. and at the same time neglecting reading and studying how to be a better person tomorrow than you are today?

g. Why is divorce so prevalent, even among professing Christians, when in Malachi 2:16 it states,' "I hate divorce." says the Lord God of Israel.' If we were to define, in one word, what God is, it is "Love". That is what He wants for us and for how we treat all others, especially our spouse. The focus that He wants for us is not to be on ourselves but to please and help others. We should take our vows seriously – till death do us part! Ephesians Chapter 5 describes what husbands and wives should do for a marriage to succeed. What child of a Christian family is ever taught this by the parents, or even do the parents knowit themselves?

15. James 4:17 says, "Anyone who knows the good he ought to do and doesn't do it, sins." How neighborly are you? Do you truly "love your neighbor as yourself", and seek how you could be encouraging and helpful?

16. And finally, the "cruncher" where we all fall short. In Luke 10:25 when Jesus was asked by an expert in the law, "What must I do to inherit eternal life?" the answer was "Love the Lord your God with all your heart and with all your soul and with all your strength and with all your mind and love your neighbor as yourself." This implies a full commitment in all your being. We are aware that the Holy Spirit is with us 24/7, in all that we do. How much of your day do you spend praying with the Spirit, totally aware that the Living Spirit is with you in all the details of the day? The average Christian spends less than 10 minutes a day in prayer and devotions, and most go on with life without ever realizing and calling on His presence in the events of the day.

In Matthew 7:21 Jesus says, "Not everyone who says to me, 'Lord, Lord,'" will enter the kingdom of heaven, but only he who does the will of my Father who is in heaven. Many will say to me in that day, 'Lord, Lord, did we not prophesy in your name, and in your name drive out demons and perform many miracles?' Then I will tell them plainly, 'I never knew you. Away from me, you evildoers!'" In other words, what is needed is a *personal relationship* seeking and discovering what His will is daily. He wants you to seek His guidance on your good deeds before you launch off on your own, as He has a plan for your efforts to succeed. You can not know what He wants you to do without consulting Him first and waiting for the answer. Why do you proceed in life as if you know and want to do it on your own?

The reason that God loves us so much and blesses us is that we might search and establish a *personal relationship* with the Living God. *He is already in you, awaiting your realization and to enthusiastically embrace The Holy Spirit*! DO IT – YOU'LL LOVE IT AND NEVER BE THE SAME!

Just as I am without one plea
And that Thou bid'st me come to thee
O Lamb of God, I come! I come.

Just as I am, though tossed about
With many a conflict, many a doubt
Fighting and fears within, without
O Lamb of God, I come! I come.

Just as I am, Thou wilt receive
Wilt welcome, pardon, cleanse, relieve
Because Thy promise I believe
O Lamb of God, I come, I come.

Song by Mahalia Jackson

CHAPTER 2
IS GOD REAL?

The basic question that we all have struggled with, "Is God real?" How can we know that He is real, in that He is unseen? If He is real, how can we know for sure? What is being taught in our schools and professed in society is that this world is the result of evolution and not creation. To believe in creation requires a belief in a creator that was there at the very beginning of time, created by the power of His being. To believe in evolution requires a belief that everything evolved from something, but this theory never. defines what the "something" was and how it was created. If you go to a junk yard, you can never find anything that has become better functionally than when it was put there. Everything that man has created is in decline. This entire debate never has a proof to it. There is only one reasonable conclusion is to take what man has used and examine it's composition and characteristics in detail, and the conclusion can only be that there had to be awsome creater that is way-beyond human explaination.

The evidence of the existence of God is overwhelming. One of the greatest miracles of all that we accept as "normal", is the miracle of life itself. From the joining of a tiny sperm and egg comes, in only nine months, a totally functioning baby with eyes to see, ears to hear, heart and blood to circulate oxygen and nutrients, hands and feet, an integrated nervous system, and a brain so complex that the largest of high-speed computers of today can not duplicate. And if, at delivery of the baby, all of this is not "normal", we assume something went wrong. And this same thing is similarly duplicated in every animal on land and every living creature in the sea.

Plants are amazing. From one single seed an oak tree eventually towering over 50 feet is created and in its lifetime, often lasting over one-hundred years, it creates millions of seeds each year with identical characteristics as to the original, only one of which can create an equivelant tree. In man's world, one and one can only make two – never more. In God's world one and one can make hundreds or even thousands. On the farm in Ohio where my book inspirations are developed, it is corn country. I once observed that the corn was especially tall that summer. I went out and measured it and found the stalks were 10 feet high. I ruminated on the fact that each stalk came from a single kernel of corn. I observed that there were at least one ear of corn on each stalk, and I counted the kernels on an average size ear and found there to be 704. That means that for God, two seeds will produce at least 1,408 kernels that are identical to the original. Such a similar multiplication occurs with every plant in all of His creation.

The heavens declare the glory of God; the skies proclaim the work of his hands.
Day by day they pour forth speech; night after night they display knowledge.
There is no speech or language where their voice is not heard. Their voice
goes out into all the earth, their words to the ends of the world.

Psalm 19:1-4

The atmosphere that we live in is a complex environment including oxygen that we need to live on. Where did it come from? We must get rid of our carbon dioxide that we generate, and plants and trees need it to create oxygen for us. Our atmosphere is uniquely created to protect us from the sun's powerful radiation. It creates moisture for clouds and rain, it cleans the pollutants that volcanoes and man cause, and creates an atmospheric pressure that life needs to exist. An amazing realization is that man still can not come up with an efficient way of turning saltwater into fresh water. Over 50% of the earth's surface is covered with saltwater. And yet God creates huge thunderstorms, rain showers, hurricanes and monsoons from moisture collected over saltwater, and all the rain from these events provide fresh water in quantities beyond man's comprehension – all from the sky! And what we see of fresh water in our lakes and streams only constitutes about 3% of all the fresh water in the world with the rest of it in underground caverns and aquifers.

Fathom this: The earth is traveling at the rate of 67,756 miles per hour around the sun, at the same time is spinning at the rate of 1,000 miles per hour at the equator. A man standing at the equator doesn't feel any different when he stands near the north pole. All of this is in perfect harmony along with the moon spinning at the rate of 10,349 mph at its equator. How did this all get created in perfect synchronization?

Every living plant and animal must have a continual source of water and nutrients, or in a matter of a few days they will die. On the farm I am surrounded by trees, full of leaves this time of the year. Consider the fact that every leaf needs water and nutrients, or in a few days it will die. For nutrients to be provided to each leaf, water must be transported to it. Where do the nutrients come from – the soil. Where does the water come from – the ground. The elements must be collected by the roots of the tree, transported *up* the trunk, (how does water flow up?), out through the limb, out on the specific branch and when it gets to the leaf it must travel through the tiny stem of the leaf before going through every part of the leaf itself. A continual supply of water and nutrients must be available from Spring until Fall every day until this supply stops in the Fall, and the leaves change color, die and fall down. And we accept these miracles as normal!

On the farm we have barn swallows – birds that are especially active during the late afternoon and evening in the summer. They fly very fast, especially over areas where mosquitoes exist. These birds feed on the mosquitoes, thank goodness, and swoop very fast to catch them. How can these birds have an eyesight capable of seeing a mosquito and catching it in fast flight? How do these birds survive in the winter when temperatures drop to well below zero degrees and there are no mosquitoes? How do some birds migrate for hundreds of miles with their tiny brains, navigating over the same routes that their ancestors have traveled for generations – even centuries? How do monarch butterflies from all over the

U.S. migrate to a single area in central America, with their tiny bodies able to propel them for hundreds of miles, through storms and bad weather?

This year will experience, in 15 states including Ohio, reemergence after 17 years *trillions* of a bug called cicada. These large, winged, kind of scary looking but mostly harmless flying insects are known for their deafening "buzz." The end of May through June, there can be hundreds of thousands in the area. They have black bodies and bold red eyes. This experience, exploding in unison every 17 years, is one of nature's great mysteries. The bugs have not been in hibernation since their last appearance in 2004. They live underground in nymph form, about a foot or two down, feeding on sap from tree roots. When the soil reaches 64 degrees Fahrenheit, they all together burrow their way to the surface and make their emergence. They climb up on the nearest thing they can find, and molt for the final time. At that time, they are white and have not developed hardened shells. After their shells develop, they are ready to look for a mate. The very loud buzzing noise comes from the male looking for a mate. After mating, females will lay eggs in soft, new twigs. The eggs hatch in six to 10 weeks, and the tiny nymphs fall to the ground and burrow in, beginning their 17-year cycle again. The cicadas are totally harmless.

How do salmon, born in rivers and streams, travel out to sea for two years and when it is time to spawn, find and endure the hardships of returning to their birthplace – up streams, up waterfalls? How can sea life exist on the underside of the ice in the Antarctic? Krill, a tiny fish, lives and propagates in such abundance under the ice that it attracts fish of all sizes to migrate each year, hundreds or even thousands of miles to feed on them. As an example, blue whales migrate as much as 6,000 miles just to feed for a few days and then find their way back to their normal habitat. How can certain birds along coastlines, especially pelicans, fly dozens of feet above the surface of a wave-swept sea with the eyesight to locate small fish to feed on, and then dive down to catch them? Where does birdlife go when hurricanes pass over, sucking up man's belongings, destroying buildings, and knocking down trees, and yet birds somehow avoid the storm and return to their normal habitat afterward?

How is it that the moon has such a gravitational pull on the earth, that its power is able to affect the seas all over the world – even on the backside of the earth away from the moon? What is gravity? Where did it come from? Without it, the earth and all it contents would cease to exist. How is it that the moon's effect on the seas is so precise that the affect of it can be predicted years in advance, allowing accurate tidal tables to be published? What is magnetism and how were the north and south poles established causing the earth to rotate about? And how is it that the poles occasionally reverse themselves, South becoming North, and North becoming South?

The earth and moon's gravitational pull caused the Apollo 11 voyage to the moon and back, to contend with some amazing unseen dynamic powers never previously experienced. Consider that the spacecraft weighed approximately 103,000 pounds. Imagine, in order to launch, enter earth's orbit, escape orbit to enter the moon's orbit, to land on the moon's surface, and reverse the process required 5,500,000 pounds of propellent on board at liftoff. The moon was nearly 240,000 miles away. The escape velocity from earth's gravitational pull required a speed of 17,500 miles per hour. In order to escape this orbit required a speed of 25,000 miles per hour. This speed was necessary in order to be able to confront the dynamic forces of gravity that are constantly changing due to the rotation of both the earth and moon. What a feat of mankind to successfully achieve this first-ever adventure, especially accomplished before digital computers were available. All of this was confronting the unseen powers working in our environment.

How is it that a ship weighing thousands of tons can float on water? How is it that an airplane weighing a million pounds or more fly - on air? How can our voice be transmitted, via telephone around the world without any interruption or delay? How can 500 people depart a Boeing 747 with telephones coming from who knows where, with all using their phones at the same time to have conversations with who and where, and not ever have a wrong number or a saturation of the phone facilities? You say these are man's innovations. And I say, they all utilize what God had already put in place, allowing man to discover what is available in His amazing creation.

Where did our sun originate with such power that it continues to burn with an intensity that lights up our entire solar system, and it seemingly had no beginning nor can be predicted to ever have an ending? And every star in the sky is a similar sun - how did they come to be? In man's study of the heavens, it has been confirmed that new galaxies are being created all the time, with suns (stars) in the center. Where does such power and matter come from? Light travels at a speed of approximately 670,000,000 miles PER HOUR. These galaxies are so far away from us that the distance away from us is measured in the time that light would travel in a *year!*

> When I consider your heavens, the work of your fingers,
> The moon and the stars, which you have set in place,
> What is man that you are mindful of him,
> The son of man that you care for him?
>
> Psalm 8:4

A galaxy is a system of billions of stars, together with gas and dust. This is all held together by gravitational attraction. Our solar system is part of the Milky Way, a thin band of light crossing the sky and is made up of faint stars. The Milky Way is estimated to have an average radius of 52,000 light years.

Figure 2-1 is a picture from a telescope in South Africa. To get this shot, the MeerKAT telescope spent 130 hours surveying the night sky with 64 dishes (some superimposed in the photograph) that were sensitive enough to pick up the huge collection of galaxies that emit light. The light was emanated from a time period known as cosmic noon, between 8 billion and 11 billion years ago. And while many of them look like mere specks, many bear similarities to the Milky Way. All of this is way more than our human minds can possibly comprehend, and yet we are led by some to believe that we live in a world the has "evolved".

The star Betelgeuse is the tenth-brightest star in the night sky. This star is 642 light years away and has a brightness of 7,500 times more than our sun, with a surface temperature of 6000 degrees Fahrenheit. The diameter of this star is 700 million miles, greater than the entire orbit of the earth around our sun.

When I contemplate all that was created untold thousands of years ago in a space that has no measurable boundaries and is still being created, I am speechless and lost in wonder, love and praise for our heavenly Father. And to think that He knows me *personally*! How can it be that He was there when I was formed in my mother's womb? It is amazing that He has included me in His book of life from my beginning until He takes me to His home in heaven. I can hardly fathom that He invites me to live forever with Him and my loved ones. I am unable to get my head around it. but He promises that it is true. (Psalm 139). Our God is so enormous and powerful that He has and continues to create galaxies, and yet He has the power and desire to know us by name, and has developed a plan for each of us individually that includes every moment of every day.

To reinforce this conviction that the earth is God's creation, go to Netflix on the internet and view any of BBC's documentaries with "Planet" in the title, such as Planet Earth, Our Planet, Blue Planet, etc. The photography is breathtaking! Although BBC occasionally mentions "evolution", the videos not only illustrate God's amazing creation they *shout* it out, in my opinion.

In the Bible in the book of Job Chapters 38 through 41, the Lord asks questions that Job and his counselors could not answer, and even with our technology and knowledge today we still can not answer them. Questions were asked of Job and his friends similar to: "Who are you that seek my council with words without knowledge? One of the few times the Lord has spoken verbally to me was in answer to my plea of "Why are you doing this?" His answer was: "Who are you to question my judgment?" I was speechless.

Where did seeds come from to start all trees and other living plants? How is it that seeds can be stored for hundreds of years in dry conditions, and come alive when water is added to them? How is it that certain trees and living plants survive a season of extreme cold conditions and then come alive in the spring? How did the design of flowers come about and continue to produce identical beauty for hundreds and thousands of years?

From what was the very first human body created, and how was it designed to function as it does? How was our brain created to control all parts of our bodily functions, to learn and store information, to remember events even from our early childhood, and to analyze and form judgments? Man is the only creature that can anticipate future events. What gave our immune system information about what to combat in order to prevent illnesses without destroying healthy tissue? How can our brain turn on and off our systems for eliminating waste fluids and solid matter? How can we see objects in an erect condition when the lenses of our eyes send the information to our brain that has the objects inverted? How can our throats properly process and send everything to the right place while we breath in oxygen and breath out carbon monoxide, talk, drink, chew, and taste all at the same time?

It is inherent in the make-up of man to search for answers to these questions. The answers are so enormous that man's mind is unable to comprehend any other conclusion other than only a God could have created what we experience in life. The Bible, book of Genesis provides the answers to all of these questions, but it takes faith to believe it because our minds are unable to comprehend the enormity of such a God with such invisible powers in which we live and move and have our being. The things in this world that we see are all temporary and eventually waste away. But the things that we must accept by faith, such as love, peace and hope - are available to us by the unseen powers that are the most valuable things in life. This Creator has placed us in this world at the greatest time in all of history! He has brought us life and breath and implanted in us a brain that I believe He wants us to use, not only to live, but to seek and contemplate Him. He knows us personally and has a plan for our life but He will not thrust it upon us – it can only be found after seeking Him and creating faith and trust in Him. He gives us something unique in His creation – a brain and complete free-will, to use it as we chose. We can continue to go our own way, or we can search and discover His plan that is a far better plan for our life. We have only one life to live on earth, and how we live it determines the quality of life while here and where we will spend eternity.

Read on in this book and be challenged by this great adventure in the unseen part of the world that we live in – the world of God the Father, His son Jesus, and the Holy Spirit; the Trinity – three in one.

> The God who made the world and everything in it is the Lord of heaven
> and earth and does not live in temples built by hands. And He is not served
> by human hands, as if He needed anything, because He himself gives all men
> life and breath and everything else. From one man He made every nation of
> men, that they should inhabit the whole earth, and He determined the times
> set for them and the exact places where they should live. God did this so that
> men would seek Him and perhaps reach out to Him and find Him, though He is
> not far from each one of us. For in Him we live and move and have our being.
> As some of our own poets have said, "We are His off-spring."
>
> Acts 17:24-28

For those who take the time and enthusiastically seek evidence of the Trinity in their life, and be willing to develop a personal relationship, the Lord promises to demonstrate His power I and offers His being in all of the details of our existence each day of our life.

CHAPTER 3
WHO IS JESUS?

This question has confronted all of mankind for over 2000 years. Jesus, when He was alive, asked his disciples: "Who do you say that I am?" No one can be convinced by anyone else or by logic – it is a matter of faith. And what is faith? It is described in the Bible, Hebrews 11:1, as "... assurance of things hoped for, a conviction of things not seen." There are two types of faith: head knowledge and heart knowledge. Most "believers" have head knowledge, they are convinced by the pure matter of overwhelming evidence of His existence as described in the Bible, and by the powerful testimonies of others who have experienced miraculous events in their lives. Scripture confirms that if you believe in Jesus and His resurrection you will receive salvation of your soul, eternal life with Him in heaven.

Is there more available to you in your walk with the Lord while here on earth? The answer to this question is "yes" – moving your faith into your heart where your spirit can be connected to His. Jesus described this event as "... being born again." This event is an individual one between you and Him in prayer, seeking Him with a sincere heart. No one can do it for you. By doing so, your spirit will be made available to Him, and He *promises* to show Himself to you. (John 14:21) Thus begins a promise that He will be with you through all of the events that you will face – both good and bad. This all occurs in the unseen world that we live in whether we realize it or not. Fix our eyes not on what is seen, but on what is unseen. For what is seen is temporary, but what is unseen is eternal. (2 Corinthians 4:18)

No amount of logic can explain love, joy, peace, patience, kindness, goodness, faithfulness, gentleness, and self-control. Can you turn tears on and off at will? What is there about a special affection for someone else? What is behind the power of forgiveness? What is it that tries your patience, but you chose to endure the hardship with confidence there will be a solution? What influences you to help others that are in need? What is it that motivates an individual to devote his or her life to become a missionary and have the confidence to travel to third-world countries where there is such an unknown future? What is it that inspires people and brings creativity to those who compose songs, or write books, or who become motivational speakers? These are all unseen events in people that logic can not define. They are all positive occurrences that we all experience without our mind and logic intentionally developing them.

What about the negative side of life? What is anger and where does it come from? Where does fear come from? Why do some people have fear and others are fearless? (Romans 8:15) What causes some people to be so violent towards people they don't even know - innocent mothers and children? Why would some bomb or shoot others and then commit suicide? How about religious belief's that are dedicated to forcing others to believe as they do, or otherwise be threatened with their lives? How is it in the spirit of a father that he would beat his wife and/or his children? What causes a loving and caring husband, married happily for many years, to cheat on his wife? What is it that, when difficulties in life occur that some people revert to drugs or alcohol? What are addictions and why are they so strong in some people that they continue with them to the point of death? These are unseen influences that are all around us in this society referred to in the Bible as sins coming from the evil spirit called Satan.

The Bible clearly states that our struggles are not so much with flesh and blood, but with the powers of the unseen world. (Ephesians 6:12) The "prince" of this world is Satan. (John 16:11) Satan tempts us all, and at the same time our greatest help is available by asking Jesus into our life to help us with our struggles. Christian bookshelves are full of books with testimonies of individuals that have experienced miraculous intervention by the power of the Lord in their life.

When Jesus was asked if he was really the Son of God, Jesus replied to consider what you have seen and heard. The blind receive sight, the lame walked, those who had leprosy cured, the deaf heard, the dead were raised, and good news was preached to the poor. In other words, judge me on what I have done miraculously. When asked what I must do to enter the kingdom of God, Jesus replied to love your God with all of your heart, with all our mind and with all you strength, and the command is also to love your neighbor as yourself. (Matthew 22:36) All of this is about loving others, not just yourself.

Scholars of the Old Testament have discovered about 600 prophecies concerning the coming of the Messiah. The story of Jesus's crucifixion is followed by hundreds of people who witnessed seeing Him in real life after His death. (Acts 1:3) He was the only person to ever have been resurrected from the dead except those few people that Jesus himself miraculously raised from the dead as a temporary reprieve. The Bible states that Jesus is the only Son of God and is the image of God in the flesh. He is loving and compassionate, wanting only the very best for His people. However, He gives us free will to decide on our own whether we accept Him in our struggles with both the seen and unseen in this world, or do we want to do it on our own?

My first book is full of testimonies of where I have experienced the Lord's presence in my walk with Him. Suffice it to say, however, that I faithfully attended and participated in church activities all my life until age 55, *not realizing that He knew me personally!* Leading up to that event, I had struggled with finding employment for 11 months but had not specifically, personally prayed asking Him for help. Finally, I went on my knees in my living room one quiet Friday morning and asked for His help in my desperate search for employment. He clearly answered this prayer, starting in a matter of less than two hours beginning with a phone call resulting 10 days later in a trip to Michigan from Florida to sign an employment agreement with a company that I had not contacted during my job search. This was so clear a response to my prayer that it changed my life completely. I had grown up with a Bible in our house, and during 32 years of marriage had accumulated several Bibles, but I had never opened the cover on even one of them. Upon my return from Michigan, I found a Bible that had been given to me by a relative 10 years prior. Although it was inscribed by the giver, I had never opened it and I did not even recall having received it. It has become my constant companion now for over 30 years, is seriously marked up and has loose pages throughout. I have separately made my own list of over 700 individual scriptural passages that I use for reference, as this list is much easier for me to find familiar passages than standard indexes. And my thirst for daily wisdom continues to this day and is now accompanied with an appreciable amount of time in meditation with our Lord Jesus and The Holy Spirit every day.

The basic questions most of us ask is why doesn't God provide unquestionable proof of His existence? The answer, I believe, is that God designed human beings with something totally unique in all of His creations; self-will, allowing us to decide *completely on our own* whether to believe in Him and in scripture or not. He has a plan for our life if we are willing to seek and be obedient to it. (Psalm 139:11) Otherwise, we would simply be robots with a pre-determined disposition. It is totally up to us, individually, as to whether to have faith and trust in Him to help us in our struggles in life, or to be totally self-determined, self-made. This subject will be discussed in greater detail in the next chapter.

What a friend we have in Jesus, all our sins and griefs to bear,
What a privilege to carry, everything to God in prayer!
O what peace we often forfeit, O what needless pain we bear,
All because we do not carry everything to God in prayer!

Have we trials and temptations, is there trouble anywhere?
We should never be discouraged, take it to the Lord in prayer.
Can we find a friend so faithful, who will all our sorrows share?
Jesus knows our every weakness, take it to the Lord in prayer.

Are we weak and heavy laden, cumbered with a load of care?
Precious Savior still our refuge, take it to the Lord in prayer.
Do thy friends despise forsake you, take it to the Lord in prayer.
In His arms He'll take and shield you, you will find a solace there.

Charles C. Converse, 1832-1918

What most Christians believe is that Jesus began His existence in the world as a baby some 2,000 years ago. Before that, where did He come from? What is little understood is that Jesus was with our Heavenly Father before the world began. Jesus Himself said, in John 17:5: "And now, Father, glorify Me in Your presence with the glory I had with you before the world began."

Jesus is referred to as "The Word" in several places in the Book of John. To begin with, in John 1:1: In the beginning was the Word, and the Word was with God, and the Word was God. He was with God in the beginning." Then in John 1:14: "The Word became flesh and made His dwelling among us. We have seen His glory, the glory of the One and Only, who came from the Father, full of grace and truth."

In John 17:24: "Father, I want those You have given Me to be with Me where I am, and to see My glory, the glory You have given Me because You loved Me before the creation of the world."

The decision is completely your own. Fully embracing Him and scripture will enormously change the remaining days of your life and will assure you of a life forever in God's heavenly kingdom. Do it – you'll like it and it doesn't cost anything!

CHAPTER 4

INTRODUCTION TO THE HOLY SPIRIT

On the last and greatest day of the Feast (Feast of Tabernacles) Jesus stood and said in a loud voice, "If a man is thirsty, let him come to me and drink. Whoever believes in Me, as the Scripture has said, streams of living water will flow from within him." By this He meant the Spirit, whom those who believed in Him were later to receive. Up to that time the Spirit had not been commonly given, since Jesus had not yet been glorified.

John 7: 37-39

Jesus stated before He was crucified that He must endure the cross in order to allow the Holy Spirit to be given to all believers, as a gift. In the Old Testament the Spirit of God was in the Saints and Prophets and intervened in others as He was directed by God but it, seemingly, was not available to everyone who believed in God. Jesus is the one who now gives the gift of the Holy Spirit to all upon our confirming a belief in Jesus' life and His resurrection. It is a gift little understood and utilized by most of Christianity. Why? We know that the Holy Spirit is part of the Trinity – three in one, all three "singing the same song." We are familiar with the Heavenly Father and with Jesus, but what of the Holy Spirit (or Holy Ghost)? The intention here in this book is to help unravel this mystery and to help readers embrace it through testimonies.

To begin, let's be clear: The Holy Spirit is given to us *believers* at the time of our declaration of belief in our Lord Jesus crucifixion and resurrection. It is personal, all knowing of our past, present, and future. It is available to help us through our difficulties, provides for our needs, and encourages us to walk the plan that Jesus has for our life. It can not and will not force us to do anything as it must work through our *free will.* He is Jesus' living spirit in us! The Trinity are totally in synch with each other. The Holy Spirit implements the instructions from our Lord Jesus, and they all three want us to seek them, learn from them, and follow their guidance to lead us on the walk that they have defined is best for us individually – if we are willing! In our prayers we can talk to any one of them at any time, and they all hear. And in John 14:21, Jesus promises that the one who loves Me will be loved by my Father, and I too will love them *and show Myself to them.* " And when He shows Himself, in any of a myriad of ways, we can take this as *confirmation of our salvation – our ticket to heaven!*

The Lord's plan for our life will not be what we expect, but if we have a willing spirit His plan will be the very best for us. We are raised up by our families, and our society encourages us to be self-sufficient, identify goals for our life, build our confidence through achieving successes, gain all the toys that we can. These are all the things of this world. However, Romans 12:1 and 2 says:

> Therefore, I urge you brothers, in view of God's mercy, to offer your
> bodies as living sacrifices, holy and pleasing to God – which is your
> spiritual worship. Do not conform any longer to the pattern of this world,
> but be transformed by the renewing of your mind. Then you will be able
> to test and approve what God's will is – His good, pleasing and perfect will.

It is important to realize that once we ask the Lord Jesus into our life, His plan will include both joys as well as guidance through guidance through all aspects of our life – the good and the bad. The hardships are where we especially are able to see Him working in our lives while teaching us what He wants us to learn. At the same time, He is helping us to live a life more worthy in preparation for acceptance into His kingdom. Learning obedience to His ways is necessary in order to experience the blessed life that He wants for us here on earth. In addition, His plan for us is not to just be a nice guy, but He wants to be able to use us as a witness as to His goodness and to encourage and help others to build their faith and trust in Him. Matthew 5:16 tells us to "Let your light shine before men, that they may see your good deeds and praise your Father in heaven."

Let's start with itemizing the attributes of the Holy Spirit that grow in us as fruit on the vine. These are love, joy, peace, patience, kindness, goodness, gentleness and self-control. These are affects that we find growing in us as we grow in our faith and trust in the Lord Jesus. These all come from the unseen world. None of these attributes can you turn on at will – you can't, through your mind, decide to love someone, or have joy, peace, etc. In addition to these attributes are additional influences that we believers experience in our relationships with others such as empathy, encouragement, sharing, hope, gladness, gratefulness, inspiration and enthusiasm. And, since we are directed to be *joyful in ALL things,* (Philippians 4:4) we are thus encouraged to be an *optimist,* to look at the positive side of life. "Accentuate the positive – eliminate the negative! Don't mess with mister in between!" as the old saying goes.

Correspondingly, there is a struggle in life with the influence from the negative side of life that we live in, referred to as sin from Satan. His attributes are hate, anger, anxiety, frustration, bitterness, fear, hopelessness, despair, depression, selfishness, arrogance, greed, violence, loneliness, sadness, constant complaining and criticizing. If you have ever struggled with any of these, it feels like a wet blanket on your spirit. These, too, are unseen influences that are readily available when the situation arises. *Our free will* is what decides the way that our mind reacts; you cannot think positive and negative thoughts at the same time – *YOU DECIDE!?*

Because all of these influences in our thinking are from the unseen world, they are often referred to as spiritual warfare. These confrontations go on individually in our very own minds – constantly, all day long and in our unconscious mind at night. All of these influences are processed through our minds for acceptance – good or bad. God never forces us to do anything, and neither can Satan. We are the gatekeeper for these unseen influences to enter into our decisions and actions. As an example, let's suppose that a car suddenly runs into the back of your car at a stoplight. What is your immediate reaction – anger, bitterness, frustration; or self-control, thankfulness to the Lord that you're not injured, concern for the other person, and a recognition that although the car is damaged it is just a "thing" as it can be repaired or replaced. This is the choice we make without having time to think – the response has already been programmed into our spirit and soul. Do we have the Holy Spirit to protect and guide us or is Satan stimulating our responses? One or the other – it can't be both.

Another aspect of the Holy Spirit in our life is the fact that it is directed by Jesus, and as such He knows everything about us – our past history in every detail, where we are with our current challenges in every minute detail, and what our future is in all detail. (Psalm 139). He even knows the decisions that we are about to make but will not force them to go His way. He knows our propensity, or inclination, in our decision making. As such, since He is working on our behalf, there are times that He is protecting us from harm whether we know it or not, even for a wrong decision leading up to it. As an example, say, we were a young man and decide to purchase and ride a motorcycle in a congested city during rush hour. This is not the action that the Lord would probably want us to take, and a pending accident is about to occur. Do we get into a serious incident or experience a near-miss? He may have saved us from a serious injury, and we didn't know it. Or possibly He allows it to be a more minor accident from which He wants us to learn a lesson. We just can't know, but the very best insurance policy in life is to develop a close relationship with our Lord where He can help our decision making. Whenever I experience something unexpected, I intentionally pray to the Lord in recognition that this situation does not come as a surprise to Him – what do you want me to learn from it? And if we are sincere about this appeal and wait Him out, He will – through the Holy Spirit – answer us in some way.

All of Satan's actions are known and allowed by Jesus before they are taken. Such an example from the Bible is the book of Job. The experience that Job had was the result of the Lord allowing Satan to do his "thing" to Job, anything except Satan could not take his life. As I see it, there were two main purposes as to why the Lord allowed it. The main purpose was to prove to everyone with knowledge of these events, the faithfulness that Job would maintain in trusting God throughout all of the ordeals – the Lord gives and the Lord takes away. The second purpose and most important one, I believe, was a rebuke to Job, family and his friends and counselors that they were speaking without wisdom. This was done by the lectures that the Lord gave them in four chapters towards the end of the book of Job. And these four chapters are equally convicting to us today, that in our age of unlimited knowledge available through the internet, we still cannot answer even one of the Lord's questions. (Job chapters 38, 39, 40 and 41). Then Job responded to the Lord: "I know that you can do all things, no plan of yours can be thwarted. You asked, "Who is this that obscures my counsel without knowledge?' Job replied, "Surely, I spoke of things I did not understand, things too wonderful for me to know."

For a proper perspective, again I repeat that our understanding should be that the event was no surprise to you Lord – what do you want me to learn from it?

This illustration is an attempt to depict the spiritual struggle that we all are experiencing.

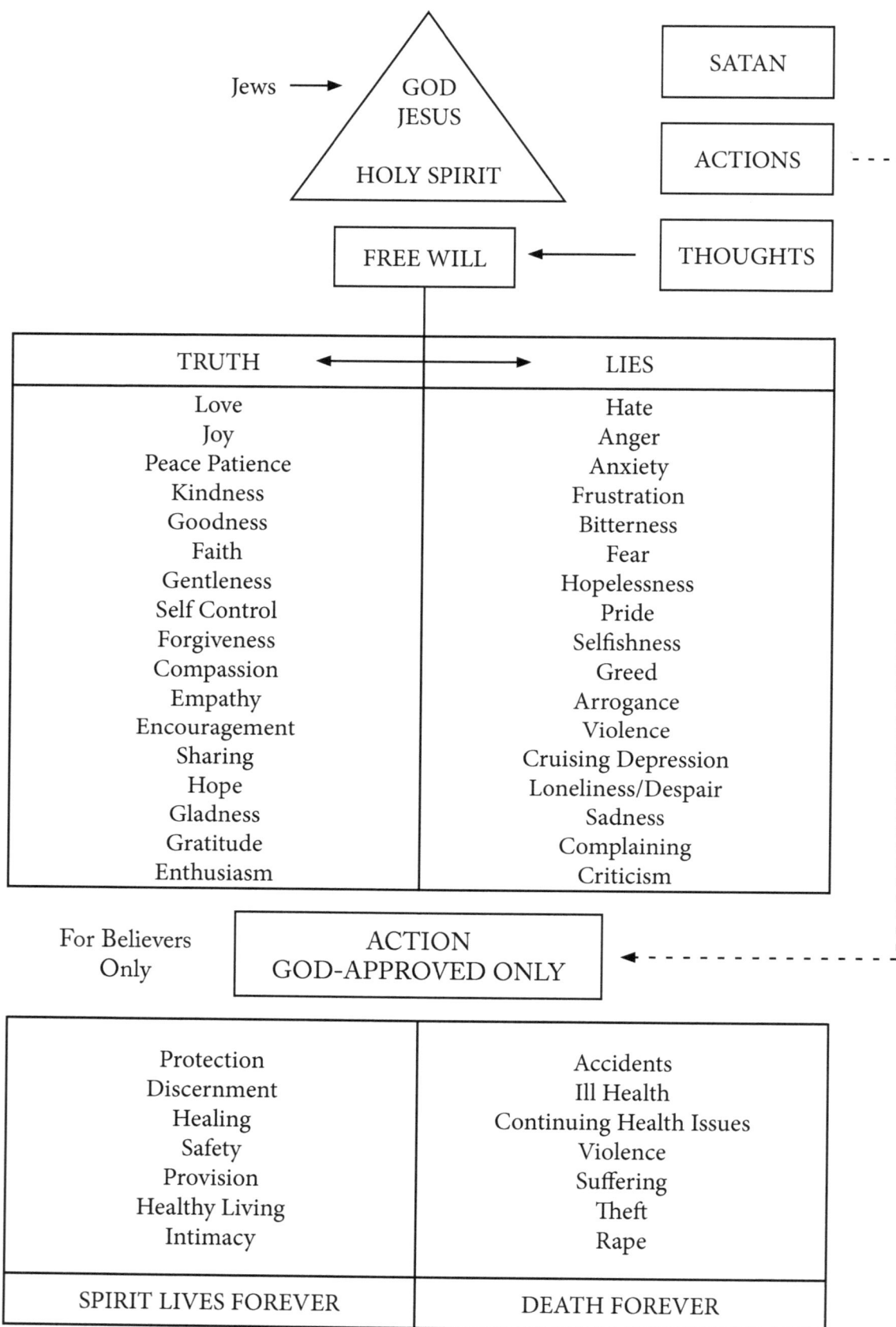

At the top is the Trinity-the three in one together in all aspects of our life – past, present and future. Our Free Will is the focal point of all that we say, think and do. If we seek the Holy Spirit, we are seeking the Truth, and the Bible is our written manual for life. This leads to the fruits of the spirit as we previously discussed. If we are not dwelling on the Trinity through the Holy Spirit in our daily events, we are exposing our free will to Satan's influence in our decisions and actions. By implanting this illustration clearly in our mind, we can better visualize and declare our opposition to Satan's attributes of frustration, anger, worry and anxiety, etc. These are in the category of "lies" that are sent to our free will, but we are not compelled to accept any of them and instead, embrace the Truth.

After over 7 years without my wife, Katie, I still fight moments of loneliness and sadness. I have consistently reminded the Lord of this but at the same time I recognize that this presents a dilemma to Him as to how this situation could be resolved without having another personal relationship with a female? After one year of being alone, He brought a very young lady of Indian descent, Pooja, to rent one of my spare bedrooms. She was more than 50 years younger than I. I had been approached by a mutual friend, Fatima, who Katie and I had helped and had known for over 20 years. Pooja had been brought to the United States through an arranged marriage, and after six months was forced to separate from her husband. She knew very little English, had not been working in the U.S., had no money, and had no family or friends here. Somehow, she had been given a car through a friend, and had a drivers' license. She was taken in by another family of the Indian culture, but was treated as an indentured servant, overworked, paid very little, and was not shown compassion. Pooja lived in the same apartment complex as Fatima but knew each other only briefly. After coming to my home, Pooja immediately got three jobs and proceeded to work 60 to 70 hours a week. In a short time, she had paid for all of her financial obligations, car insurance, an iPhone, room rent and had money to spare. This brought her great joy and great appreciation for being able to stay in my home and to live as an American. For me, she brought activity in the home and referred to me as her American father, with a hug every time she saw me. She also stated that she appreciated my desire to help others in need. She had observed that the American Christian spirit showed more love and compassion in helping others than they had in their culture in helping even family members. And, in addition, the Lord brought me activities in my home to help with my loneliness. Thank you, Lord! What an unusual way to help me deal with my loneliness!

After living nearly three years in my home, she was again married through arrangement by her family in India and moved to Tennessee to be with her husband. In the meantime, Fatima had lost her husband and was struggling with minimum-wage jobs trying to meet living expenses. I offered Fatima to use my other spare bedroom and she came just before Pooja moved out. And recently Fatima's son, Xavior, moved into Pooja's old bedroom as he is going through some hard times. So, the Lord has answered my prayers in such an unusual way, helping with expenses and at the same time helping me to cope with my loneliness. At the same time, this was providing needed help to each or them. None of this was planned for by anyone – instead, it was orchestrated by our Loving and caring Lord Jesus.

Regarding the physical aspect of our life, the bottom of Figure 3-3 depicts what we are experiencing. As previously discussed, Satan has no ability to impact us directly without first the knowledge and approval of the Trinity. In other words, Satan cannot act on his own with accidents, ill health, etc. without the Lord knowing and interceding as He sees is appropriate for the outcome to conform to His plan for our life. And when our days on earth are over, we will experience either that our spirit lives forever or dies forever.

If we want to live fullness of life, then seek and follow the plan that our Lord Jesus has made uniquely for each of us. Otherwise, Satan will aggravate our life on earth, and we will experience his consequences for the rest of our life.

SPIRIT SONG

Oh, let the Son of God enfold you with His Spirit and His love,
Let Him fill your heart and satisfy your soul,
Oh, let Him have the things that hold you, and His Spirit like a dove,
Will descend upon your life and make you whole.
Jesus, O Jesus, come and fill your lamb.

Oh, come and sing the song with gladness, as your hearts are filled with joy,
Lift your hands in sweet surrender to His name,
Oh, give Him all your tears and sadness, give Him all your years of pain,
And you'll enter into life in Jesus name.

Jesus, O Jesus, come and fill your lamb,
Oh, let the Son of God enfold you with His Spirit and His love,
Let Him fill your heart and satisfy your soul,
And you'll enter into life in Jesus name.

Song Writer: Wimber John Richard
For a real treat, Google Spirit Song,
And select The Maranatha! Singers

CHAPTER 5
WHAT IS A CHRISTIAN RE-VIVAL?

Revival refers to a spiritual reawakening from a state of dormancy or stagnation in the life of a believer. It encompasses the resurfacing of a love for God, an appreciation of God's holiness, a passion for His Word and His church, a convicting awareness of personal and corporate sin, a spirit of humility, and a desire for repentance and growth in righteousness. Revival invigorates and sometimes deepens a believer's faith opening his or her eyes to the truth in a fresh new way. It generally involves the connotation of a fresh start with a clean slate marking a new beginning of a life lived in obedience to God. Revival breaks the charm and power of the world which blinds the eyes of men and generates both the will and power to live in the world but not of the world.

In the USA, the first revival, also called the First Great Awakening, produced an upsurge of devotion among Protestants in the 1730's and 1740's, carving a permanent mark on American religion. It resulted from authoritative preaching that deeply moved the church members with a convicting awareness of personal guilt and the awesome nature of salvation through Christ. Breaking away from dry ritual and rote ceremony, the Great Awakening made Christianity intensely personal to the average person, as it should be, by creating a deep emotional need for relationship with Christ. 2:10-11

Revival, in many respects, replicates the believer's experience when he or she is saved, it is initiated by a prompting of the Holy Spirit, creating an awareness of something missing or wrong in the believer's life that can only be righted by God. In turn the Christian must respond from the heart, acknowledging his or her need. Then in a powerful way, the Holy Spirit draws back the veil the world has cast over the truth, allowing the believers to fully see themselves in comparison to God's majesty and holiness. Obviously, such comparisons bring great humility, but also great awe of God and His truly amazing grace (Isaiah 6:7) . Unlike the original conversion experience that brings about a new relationship to God, however, revival represents a restoration of fellowship with God, the relationship having been retained even though the believer had pulled away for a time.

God, through His Holy Spirit, calls us to revival in a number of situations. Christ's letters to the seven churches reveal some circumstances that may necessitate revival. In the letter to Ephesus, Christ praised the church for their perseverance and discernment but He stated that they had forsaken their first love (Revelation 2:4-5). Many times as the excitement of acceptance to Christ grows cold, we lose the zeal that we had at first. We become bogged down in the ritual going through the motions, and we no longer experience the joy of serving Christ. Revival helps restore that first love and passion for Christ. Revelation 2:10-11 refers to the church at Smyrna, which was suffering intense persecution. The cares and worries of life can beat us down, leaving us emotionally, physically, and spiritually exhausted. Revival can lift us up to new hope and faith.

Revelation 2:14-16 talks about the problem of compromise with the world and incorporating worldly values into our belief systems. Revival helps us to rightly discern what values we should hold. Revelation 2:20-23 discusses the problem of tolerating false teaching in our churches. We need to examine the messages that we hear and compare them to the message of the Bible. Revival helps us to find the truth. Revelation 3:1-6 describes a dead church that goes through the motions outwardly, but there is nothing underneath. Here is a picture of nominal Christianity, outwardly prosperous, busy with the externals of religious activity, but devoid of spiritual life and power. Revival helps to resuscitate spiritual life. In Revelations 3:11, we are further warned against complacency, a life that does not bear fruit. All of these scenarios call for revival.

The evidence of revival, a great outpouring of the Holy Spirit upon believers is changed lives. Great movements toward righteousness, evangelism, and social justice occur. Believers are once again spending time in prayer and reading and obeying God's Word. Believers begin to powerfully use their spiritual gifts. There is confession of sin and repentance.

As this chapter is being written, revival has recently broken out at Asbury University and Texas A&M.

Google – February 20, 2023

Copyright Got Questions Ministries

CHAPTER 6
THE HOLY SPIRIT IN OUR DAILY LIFE

In order to help us be sensitive to the daily presence of the Holy Spirit in our lives, Psalm 139 provides a wonderful summary to be embraced enthusiastically. The more that we become aware that *He is truly in our life at all times,* the more we appreciate His help under all circumstances. We tend to believe that the Holy Spirit only came to be as a result of Jesus' resurrection. In actuality, the Spirit is referenced multiple times in the Old Testament, especially in the Psalms as clearly emphasized in Psalm 139.

Psalm 139 (NIV)

O Lord, you have searched me and you know me,

You know when I set and when I rise; you perceive my thoughts from afar.

You discern my going out and my lying down; You are familiar with all my ways.

Before a word is on my tongue You know it completely, O Lord. You hem me in, behind and before.

Such knowledge is too wonderful for me, too lofty for me to attain.

COMMENTS

This clearly confirms that He knows everything that is going on in our life from morning to morning, wherever we are, and even knows what we are planning to do and why. There is nowhere that we can hide. When we pray it is like we are talking to Him as He is in us every moment.

Words that we express are very important, both good and bad. Words can either hurt or help others, and they can either hurt or help our relationship with the Lord.

This is so astonishing, and it is the greatest understanding that we can have to change all aspects of our life. The creator of the world knows us personally and is with us at all times.

Where can I go from Your Spirit?
Where can I flee from Your presence?
If I go up to the heavens, You are there,

Whenever I am flying, I often pray "Holy Spirit, demonstrate your presence, and at that time I can sense His Spirit within me.

If I make my bed in the depths,
You are there

In our family live-aboard sailboat that we have had for 40 years, the bed is below the waterline, and He has kept us safe through many storms and perilous situations.

If I rise on the wings of the dawn,
if I settle on the far side
of the sea, You are there,
even there Your hand will
guide me, Your right hand
will hold me fast.

During our five trips to the Bahama's and two summers sailing from Florida to the Upper Peninsula of Michigan, we experienced many storms, but were always kept safe, and often felt the Lord's presence. One storm was very significant.

If I say "Surely the darkness will
hide me and the light become
night around me," even the
darkness will not be dark
to You. The night will shine
like the day, for darkness is
as light to You.

I definitely felt "guided" into a sheltered area, one that I could not even find on the chart. The storm hit in the dark about 11:00 PM and was buffeted by the wind so bad that the boat sailed back and forth on the anchors. The next day I found that one of the anchors was buried so deep that I could not raise it, so I had to cut the rope. We then learned that the previous night a large sailboat in an annual race in Lake Michigan. on the other side of the lower part of Michigan, capsized and a life was lost – the first time in over 100 years in the history of the race.

For You created my inmost being;
You knit me together in my mother's womb.
I praise You because I am fearfully and wonderfully
made; Your works are wonderful;
I know that full well.

This speaks to the sanctity of life. The Lord formed you to be as you are, to be healthy and whole. If you had a defect at birth, He allowed it for His reasons. To be fearfully made is to have an understanding that He allows consequences for the decisions that we or our parents made that are not in His will such as the living conditions that you were brought up under.

My frame was not hidden from you when
I was made in the secret place.
When I was woven together in the depths of the earth,
Your eyes saw my unformed body.

He formed us to be just as we were at birth. He knew you personally, and nothing was a surprise to Him. Our environment however, such as drugs, alcohol, smoking, or viruses He may allow to affect our health while being developed before birth. Such decisions may have consequences.

All the days ordained for me were written
In Your book before one of them came to be.

Ordained or conferred on you – and as a believer in our Lord Jesus, He has plans for your life, already written in His book of life. What do you think that He has written about you as a result of your commitment to walk a closer walk with Him?

How precious to me are Your thoughts, O God. How vast is the sum of them! Were I to count them they would outnumber the grains of sand.

Until we realize that the Holy Spirit is in our every thought, we assume that our thoughts are our own. Once we fully realize that He is feeding His thoughts to us, we can begin to make better decisions, especially when we are praying in the Spirit. This is one of the primary ways that He communicates us, but we must be living with an awareness that the Spirit is in us at all times and wants you to call on Him.

When I awake I am still with You.

It is important to make your first thought of the day a recognition that the Holy Spirit is present and awaiting to communicate. Be grateful for how you have already been blessed. Be aware that He already knows what your day will be like, and that you want Him to be with you in every thought, word and deed throughout the day. Also, be thankful that the Lord Jesus has died for you and has given you the gift of the Holy Spirit.

If only You would slay the wicked, O God!
Away from me you bloodthirsty men!
They speak of You with evil intent;
Your adversaries misuse Your name.

Be aware that the Prince of this world is satan. Jesus will save us when He comes again. Therefore, satan is lurking throughout this dark world and be aware of it in your daily life. Swearing and foul language has become all too commonplace and our words define us. You should never use His name in vain. The Holy Spirit is listening!

Do I not hate those who hate You O Lord,
and abhor those who rise up against You?
I have nothing but hatred for them;
I count them my enemies.

We are confronted with this every day, and our society is pressuring us to accept those who want to destroy Christianity or suppress it, such as our government and schools. The important part that you must play is to clarify with the Holy Spirit where you stand in this spiritual warfare, to let HIm help fight your battles, and to lead you in what part He wants you to play in this struggle. Do not blindly ignore the rampant war against our freedom to worship, as clearly defined by the U.S. Constitution.

Search me, O God, and know my heart.
Test me and know my anxious thoughts.
See if there is any offensive way in me,
and lead me in the way everlasting.

This should be the daily pleading of your heart, for you are never going to be perfect in the eyes of our Lord. He will respond to your desire to walk a closer walk with Him, slowly working in your life to refine your ways.

THE SPIRIT SONG

Holy Spirit, rain down, rain down
O Comforter and Friend
How we need Your touch again
Holy Spirit, rain down, rain down.

Let Your power fall
Let Your voice be heard
Come and change our hearts
As we stand on Your word
Holy Spirit rain down, rain down!

No eye has seen, no ear has heard
No mind can know what God has in store,
So, open up Heaven, open it wide
Over Your church and over our lives,
Holy Spirit, rain down.

Source: Musixmatch Songwriters: Russell Fragar

CHAPTER 7
WHAT THE BIBLE SAYS ABOUT THE HOLY SPIRIT

A very common misunderstanding among believers is that the Holy Spirit was introduced for the first time by Jesus, when He said that He needed to be crucified in order that God would send the Holy Spirit to us. I find it important to clarify this misunderstanding by pointing out the *many scriptural passages* in both the Old and New Testament before Pentecost.

OLD TESTAMENT

1. The first time that God's spirit is mentioned is in the very first paragraph of Genesis 1:1 and 2 – In the beginning God created the heavens and the earth. Now the earth was formless and empty, darkness was over the surface of the deep, and the Spirit of God was hovering over the waters. (Notice the capital letter "S")

    The next time was in Genesis 6:3 – The Flood – When men began to increase in number on the earth and daughters were born to the them, the sons of God saw that the daughters of men were beautiful, and they married any of them they chose. Then the Lord said, "My Spirit will not contend with man forever, for he is mortal, his days will be a hundred and twenty years."

2. David has many references to the Spirit beginning in Psalm 104:24 – How many are your works, O Lord! In wisdom You made them all; the earth is full of Your creatures. There is the sea, vast and spacious, teeming with creatures beyond number – living things both large and small. There the ships go to and fro, and the leviathan, which You formed to frolic there. These all look to You to give them food at the proper time. When You give it to them, they gather it up, when You open Your hand, they are satisfied; when You hide Your face, they are terrified; when You take away their breath, they die, and return to the dust. When You send Your Spirit, they are created, and You renew the face of the earth.

And there is my favorite Psalm from David, 139, that addresses the fact that he cannot go anywhere but what the Spirit is there. I have already discussed this Psalm in detail in the previous chapter.

David again references it in Psalm 143:10 – Teach me to do Your will, for You are my God, may Your good Spirit lead me on level ground.

3. Isaiah references the Spirit many times, beginning in Chapter 11: 1-5:

A shoot will come up from the stump of Jesse, from his roots a Branch will bear fruit. The Spirit of the Lord will rest on him – the Spirit of wisdom and of understanding, the Spirit of counsel and of power, the Spirit of knowledge and of the fear of the Lord – and he will delight in the fear of the Lord.

And in Chapter 3:1 – Woe to the obstinate children, declares the Lord, to those who carry out plans that are not by My Spirit, heaping sin upon sin.

In Chapter 32:14 and :15 – The fortress will be abandoned, the noisy city deserted; citadel and watchtower will become a wasteland forever the delight of donkeys, a pasture for flocks, until the Spirit is poured upon us from on high, and the desert becomes a fertile field, and the fertile field seems like a forest.

Chapter 34:16. In speaking of desert animals says, "Look in the scroll of the Lord and read: 'None of these will be missing, not one will lack her mate. For it is His mouth that has given the order, and His Spirit will gather them together. He allots their portion, His hand distributes them by measure."

In Chapter 61:1, Isaiah says, "The Spirit of the Sovereign Lord is on me, because the Lord has anointed me to preach to the poor."

In Chapter 63:10, Isaiah is speaking about the good things that the Lord has done for the house of Israel, "Yet they rebelled and grieved the Holy Spirit."

4. In Ezekiel Chapter 2:1, referring to God: "He said to me, 'Son of man, stand up on your feet and I will speak to you.' As he spoke, the Spirit came into me and raised me to my feet, and I heard Him speaking to me."

5. In the book of Joel Chapter 2:28, the Lord says: "And afterward, I will pour out My Spirit on all people. Your sons and daughters will prophesy, your old men will dream dreams, and your young men will see visions."

6. Micah 2:7 says: "Is the Spirit of the Lord angry? Does He do such things?" "Do not my words do good to him whose ways are upright?"

7. And finally, in Zechariah, several references are to the Spirit. Chapter 4:6 says, "So he said to me, 'This is the word of the Lord to Zerubbabel: Not by might nor by power, but by My Spirit, says the Lord Almighty."
In Chapter 6:8, "Then he called to me, 'Look, those going toward the north country have given My Spirit rest in the land of the north."

In concluding the Old Testament, ponder the following thoughts:

The Holy Spirit performs the tasks that God decides and Jesus directs, even in the times before Jesus was introduced into the world as a child. As examples:

a. He performed the events that made Moses special, conducted the plagues, provided the guidance and provisions (daily water and manna). Parted the Red Sea, and provided encouragement and guidance during the exodus.

b. He provided the personal direction for Jonah to be a prophet.

c. He directed the experiences in Joshuha's life culminating in the battle of Jericho that brought down the walls.

d. He chose David to be special in the eyes of God, encouraged him to fight and kill Goliath, orchestrated all the events in David's life.

e. He was the power and wisdom in Solomon's life.

f. He developed the circumstances in Job's life and trials.

These Old Testament characters were the human instruments, and the Holy Spirit was the agent of God.

NEW TESTAMENT

The New Testament has numerous references to the Holy Spirit before the Spirit was powerfully on display at Pentecost in Acts Chapter 2.

1. In Matthew 1:18 it says: "This is how the birth of Jesus Christ came about: His mother Mary was pledged to be married to Joseph, but before they came together, she was found to be with child through the Holy Spirit.

   In Chapter 3:11, John the Baptist says: "I baptize you with water for repentance. But after me will come one who is more powerful than I, Whose sandals I am not fit to carry. He will baptize you with the Holy Spirit . . . "

   In Chapter 12:17, Jesus quoted what was spoken through the prophet Isaiah about the coming Messiah: "Here is My servant whom I have chosen, the one I love, in whom I delight. I will put My Spirit on him, and He will proclaim justice to the nations."

2. In Mark 1:8, John the Baptist proclaims regarding the one who comes after me: "I baptize you with water, but He will baptize you with the Holy Spirit."

3. In Chapter 12;35, "While Jesus was teaching in the temple courts, he asked, "How is it that the teachers of the law say that the Christ is the son of David? David himself, speaking by the Holy Spirit, declared:

> "The Lord said to my Lord: Sit at My right hand until I put your enemies under Your feet."

4. Luke refers many times to the Holy Spirit before the Pentecost, beginning in Chapter 1:15, when discussing the Prophet Zechariah when the angel of the Lord appeared to him and said: "Do not be afraid, Zechariah; your prayer has been heard. Your wife Elizabeth will bear you a son, and you are to give him the name John. He will be a joy and delight to you, and many will rejoice because of his birth, for he will be great in the sight of the Lord. He is never to take wine or other fermented drink, and he will be filled with the Holy Spirit even from birth."

In Luke 1:34, "How will this be", Mary asked the angel, "since I am a virgin?" The angel answered, "The Holy Spirit will come upon you, and the power of the Most High will overshadow you."

Other scripture in the Book of Luke referring to the Holy Spirit before Pentecost are:

1:67	4:1
2:26	4:14
3:16	4:18
3:22	11:13

5. The Book of John also has numerous mentions of the Holy Spirit before Pentecost:

1:32 thru :34	14:15
3:5 and :6	14:26
3:34	15:26
6:63	16:7
7:39	

The greatest example of the power of the Holy Spirit is what impact Pentecost had on the disciples. It was clear that Jesus' teachings gave the disciples head knowledge but was not spiritually impacting. They continually showed that they were clueless. In addition, they were unschooled, ordinary men. Acts Chapter 2 begins: "When the day of Pentecost came, they were all together in one place. The Holy Spirit came with a violent wind and what seemed to be tongues of fire, separated and rested on each of them. All were filled with the Holy Spirit and began to speak in tongues as the Spirit enabled them. At the time there were Jews from every nation under heaven that heard them speaking in tongues along with the wind that everyone heard and were perplexed. Then Peter stood up with the eleven, raised his voice and addressed the crowd. His speech was so impacting that about 3,000 became believers that day." And thus, each of the disciples were spiritually inspired to preach the gospel and write the books in the New Testament, beginning what is now known as Christianity.

The impact of the Holy Spirit on the disciples is the clearest examples of being born again - Radically changed lives!

CHAPTER 8
HOW THE HOLY SPIRIT GETS INVOLVED

Jesus Calling (daily devotional):

I speak to you continually. My nature is to communicate, though not always in words. I fling glorious sunsets across the sky, day after day. I speak in the faces and voices of loved ones. I caress you with a gentle breeze that refreshes and delights you. I speak softly in the depths of your spirit, where I have taken up residence.

You can find Me in each moment, when you have eyes to see and ears that hear. Ask My spirit to sharpen your spiritual eyesight and hearing. I rejoice each time you discover My presence. Practice looking and listening for Me during your quiet intervals. Gradually you will find Me in more and more of your moments. You will seek Me and find Me when you seek Me above all else.

"Jesus Calling" book by Sarah Young
June 20

Remember, the Holy Spirit is part of the Trinity and is the living God in you with all of the power, innovation and creativity of the Creator Himself because He and the Creator are one along with Jesus. He knows your prayers, knows your needs, and is aware of the desires of your heart because *He lives in you at all times, day and night!* He knows the plan the Lord has just for you *in detail* but you cannot know it unless you seek Him with all of your heart. And when you receive an answer to your prayer or concern, you will rarely find it in a way that you have anticipated, as His way is better and He delights in showing you that He is involved. In this way, the answer will bring assurance and joy to you that you are not alone in the events of your life – even in the smallest of details.

We are not alone in our daily endeavors as our lives are part of an intricate web with other people that we may or may not know - but He does. As an example, I had a solar panel installed on my home in

Florida last year. The system was a bit delayed and was not completed until after I had flown to Ohio for the summer. Karen McDonnald, a customer support representative for the solar company, was assigned to stand in for me in my absence and to answer questions that I might have. As a result, we had several discussions via phone, although at the time of this writing I had never met her in person. During these telephone conversations, we always ended up with a spiritual discussion about our understandings and experiences during our individual walk with our Lord. I found that she is extremely mature in her faith and is pretty much on "the same page" as I am spiritually. Therefore, I invited her to tell her stories of faith, and have included them in three chapters in this book. I have also included the testimonies of others that I have found inspiring.

Another great example of how the Holy Spirit has had a plan that has been underway for years, is this writing sanctuary in Ohio where I am blessed with to compose this book. Memories of this home date back to when I was in high school between junior and senior years – 70 years ago. This house was a very old house with less than 800 square feet of living space. One of my jobs as a teenage hired hand was to help destruct the inside, tearing out the old plaster walls and stairway to the second floor. It was about to go through a complete makeover for Calvin and Barb Canfield, the family that owned the farm, who were just married a few months prior. They were living with his parents across the country road in a house that was initially constructed in 1863. The home that I am now living in became Cal and Barb's home and was where I met Barb's sister Katie, who six years later became my wife. Katie's father had died a year earlier, her mother had just given up their home in Ann Arbor and became a housemother in a men's dormitory at the University of Michigan, where she then resided permanently. Katie, at that time was without a home, and this farmhouse eventually was where she planted roots. She did, however, spend her senior year in her hometown, St. John's, Michigan, living with friends of the family. She was born in St. John's where she had spent her first eight years, and still had good friends there. For the next six years, Katie and I never lived in the same town together but used this home on the farm where we courted during holidays and vacations. Throughout our married life, we spent innumerable times here while our families were growing up. Memories of loving times abound here and is partially the reason why I can feel so blessed and inspired by the Lord to do my creative writing in this home after all these years of memories. To me, this home is clearly where the Lord planned for me to be as a writing sanctuary for my new career, writing about Him while reflecting on my love, experiences and wisdom from the past. I can sense His Holy Spirit throughout each day, inspiring me and demonstrating His presence in daily happenings. I can dwell on His presence, feel His inspiration, and allow His thoughts to help develop this publication in a way that He wants it presented. What exciting thoughts to ponder!

He sometimes communicates to me with words directly. I have occasionally experienced this miraculous method of communication. One such event occurred while singing in our choir in Tampa at an Easter Cantata. During a break between songs while narration was in process, I looked out at our son, Bob, who was a teenager and not active in church activities. As I looked at him, the Holy Spirit said: "Bob is My responsibility, and I have plans for him." I was speechless! It was clear that it was from the Lord, and no one else heard it! I will never forget the exact words, and it changed my relationship with Bob, from a father influencer to a friend. Through the years, I have again heard His voice on different occasions, and if you ever experience it, there will be no question who's voice it is,. You will never forget the exact words, and it is always relevant to what is going on. Such a similar type of communication is rare for some people, but there are others who hear His voice often. His voice is usually very soft and our minds need to be at peace and open for us to hear Him.

He occasionally speaks through others with words that He puts on their heart or in their mind to express to others. This often comes through encouragement or suggestions from our friends, or from a Sunday sermon. As an example, last year I was struggling very hard to establish on-line banking so that I might manage my banking activities in Tampa while residing in Ohio. I needed to incorporate this capability in my laptop computer so that my friend living in my home in Tampa could deposit her monthly rent payment to me directly from her bank account into mine in a different bank. As a further complication, she wanted to do it from her smart phone in Florida, and I was not able to have an internet connection for my IPhone in the farm-country of Ohio. A friend nearby in Ohio was determined to resolve this issue for me. After multiple discussions 2 ½ hours on the phone and the internet, she finally resolved the problems. My friend in Tampa then declared that my friend in Ohio was clearly an angel that the Lord sent to help us, and I completely agreed with her.

Fast forward now a year and I am back here in Ohio for the next summer, intending to finish this book. At my age especially, when I resolve a technical issue I usually move on to other challenges, and it is easy for me to forget the resolution to past struggles. This summer I was again challenged with the same on-line banking dilemma. I totally forgot that I already had the on-line banking app installed. After four days of trying to install the app, my computer kept frustrating me asking for my "user name" and "password". I had totally forgotten that I had established them the previous summer. In frustration, I called the bank that confirmed that they knew both of these names and they even recognized my voice but they could not give them to me "for security purposes". I confirmed my identity as the account holder, but their "protocol" prevented them from giving it to me. I then elevated the dilemma to the bank Director of Customer Service, who also refused me. So, I gave up for the day and admitted to the Lord in a conversation that I had prayed for days for a resolution to the issue. I knew that He would help resolve this issue, and I knew that He wanted me to be patient. As a way to relieve my frustration, I decided, after dinner, to proof read more of this book that I had written the previous year. And what I discovered was that I had written about this same challenge the previous year. In thinking through what was going on with the bank previously, I went to a file folder that I had brought to Ohio, and behold the user name and password were written on the front of the folder – and they worked!! I have to give the Holy Spirit credit for resolving this issue as I would have never remembered it on my own.

The most common way that the Holy Spirit seems to want to communicate to us is through our thoughts. Often, as we struggle for a resolution to a situation, our thoughts are scrambled as we attempt to find the best solution with the options that we know of. What we are missing, however, are the options that He knows about that are not revealed to us because we are totally concentrating on our own approach to the problem. The very best solution is to train our mind to stop worrying and struggling for the answer. Instead, we should give the problem over to the Lord totally and completely, stop setting a time limit, and focus on seeking His answer. He always has the perfect solution – even to complex technical issues. When we cease struggling, His thoughts can better be communicated to us.

As another example, I recently panicked realizing that I had inadvertently deleted a significant part of this chapter that I knew was very much inspired by Him. I have been very frustrated with this version of Microsoft Word that was the latest and (supposedly) the greatest, as it is much too complex and sophisticated for me to ever learn on my own. Besides, I really don't need any of these sophistications – I only need and want basic word processing features. I then decided to take a break and go out and pull weeds in my flower bed while I cooled down from my anxiety and process my loss. As I came back to the computer, the thought came to me to talk to my friend and computer guru in Tampa to get his advice. He suggested that I purchase a program from Microsoft of the last version of the word processing program that I was comfortable and familiar with. This I did that turned out to be a version that was 14 years earlier. A good friend here in Ohio was able to install it and refine and explain the features to this program to me, and I am very pleased with it. Regarding the lost writings that were gone permanently, I believed that the Holy Spirit was telling me that He was wanting me to rewrite this section.

Another current example from last year is regarding my brother, Neil, who was facing multiple serious issues with his health. He lived in the upper part of Michigan, about 300 miles away. One of my other brothers lives nearby here in Ohio, and we both traveled up to see Neil for a brief visit as he was in the hospital. A day or two later when we needed to return back to Ohio, my prayer was for the Lord to tell me when the best time for me to return would be as I realized that he was nearing his last day. When we saw him, he had been placed on an oxygen mask to help his breathing in the emergency room, but then later it was determined that this was considered life support and that was against Neil's wishes. When this happened, the plan was then to transport him to a Hospice home where the oxygen mask was to be removed. For some reason, my spirit helped me decided to travel three days later. To myself I questioned why I added an extra day but decided that it was for a reason that I could not account for. As it turned out, I was desperately needed to resolve the banking/computer issue discussed above. In addition, Neil was comfortable in the Hospice home with his oxygen mask removed. When my banking issue was resolved, the next morning I traveled to the Hospice home and arrived within an hour of Neil's last breath.

This last year at my home in Tampa I changed mobile phone companies in order to experience a significant reduction in costs. Prior to that decision, I checked with the new company to have them verify that there was service at this address in Ohio, and I was assured that there was. Now that I am here, yes there is a signal, but it is too weak to be reliable. In addition, for the several years that I have been coming here in the summers, I never have had internet service. I would have to go into town to the library, six miles away, or go to my friend's business 15 miles away. My nephew across the country road about 100 yards away has internet/wi-fi, but I cannot pick it up inside my house. To have direct service to my home would cost $79 per month on a one-year contract. I'm only here for four months so that is not going to happen. My evening loneliness at home is resolved by watching Netflix, but this summer I do not have it available in the house. The thought (thank you Holy Spirit) came to me to explore the outside of the house for wi-fi from my nephew, and I found that I am able to barely get it by setting in the garage. That is not the most convenient, but it works except when mosquitoes are around. I was considering getting window screen material that I could temporarily add in the doorway while I sat there on a lawn chair in the evenings. Then, in my time of meditating with the Lord, the thought came to go on the internet to see it there is such a thing as a signal amplifier and, sure enough, there was one that I could purchase for $109 that would give me my own wi-fi hot spot in the house for my IPhone, IPad and laptop. Hallelujah! And it is portable so that I could also take it to my brother in rural South Carolina when I am visiting. I have learned through many years of experience that my most innovative times come as I am in prayer and meditation in bed before I get up in the morning– often as long as 45 minutes as I review, with the Holy Spirit, what is going on in my life. It is amazing what comes to mind!

> When I am down, and, oh my soul, so weary
> When troubles come, and my heart burdened be
> Then, I am still and wait here in the silence
> Until you come and sit awhile with me.
>
> You raise me up, so I can stand on mountains.
> You raise me up to walk on stormy seas.
> I am strong when I am on your shoulders
> You raise me up to more that I can be

Song by Josh Groban
For a treat, Google "You Raised Me Up"

CHAPTER 9
EXPERIENCING THE HOLY SPIRIT IN CAR ISSUES

Since I have been a do-it-yourselfer nearly all of my life, and mostly driving well-used cars, having a mechanical issue is not unusual for me. When someone ran into my beloved red Mercury Cougar and destroyed it, I couldn't get a loan for another newer car as I recently started my own business, working for commissions. Having no past history of commissions I had to purchase an older car with the cash that I had available. And now, in retrospect, I have come to realize the saving grace of the Lord as a result of it, giving me testimonies that I can now share as well as saving an untold amount of money on depreciation, loan interest and insurance premiums. This further proves the point that the Holy Spirit knows how to make lemonade out of the lemons in our life, fitting into a plan that is certainly not of our choosing.

My first book, Grandpa's Walk with The Lord, describes many experiences that make this point, and I will not repeat them. I am now the owner/user of three cars – the youngest is my car at my Florida home, a 20 years old Oldsmobile Alero. It is a bright red sports-type that runs great, makes me feel young and has plenty of power when I need (or want) it. It currently has 218,000 miles but runs beautifully with minimum maintenance costs and is extremely comfortable. It was given to me by my daughter six years ago after her daughters grew up using it. Since I am living on Social Security plus a very small annuity, I am not anxious to spring for a newer car if I don't have to. The year before the Lord took my wife, Katie, to heaven, we drove her nice 1990 (30 years old) Ford LTD Crown Victoria to Ohio to be used in the summertime so that we could fly back and forth from Florida. In the wintertime it is stored in a barn on the family farm where Katie's sister, Barb, lived until last year when the Lord had her join Katie in Heaven. Barb's car is licensed and insured by her son who lives across the country road, as he wants to keep it operation, so he wants me to use it when I come up in the summer. It is a 1998 Buick – now a 22-year-old car. All three of these I drive without reluctance as I depend on the Holy Spirit to warn me of any issues that need to be addressed before I travel any distance. And then I depend on Him to show me any solutions to issues should any come up along the way. Otherwise, I do not fret or worry about my transportation.

Last summer during my four-month stay in Ohio, I used my beautiful Crown Victoria for longer trips. One trip was to Grand Rapids, Michigan, to take my sailboat outboard motor to be tuned up. This was a four-hour trip one way. I always pray earnestly before and during such a trip, for Him to help me along the way. I had absolutely no sign of a problem both going and coming, eight hours of driving, until I was within two miles of home on the farm. As I turned to go down the country road at the end of the journey, the engine stopped, and I was barely able to glide to a gravel driveway. It would not start so I opened the hood to see if there was anything obviously wrong. I immediately detected that it was overheating from lack of enough water, and the temperature warning gauge was not working. I always carry two gallons of water in the trunk just in case I need them.

I used both of them just to cool down the radiator. I then realized I did not have any water to fill up the radiator and the car would overheat before going the two remaining miles. What to do now? It was nearly dark, and I could hardly see what I was doing. I suddenly realized that there was a pond on the other side of the farmhouse. All I had to do was refill the two gallons, and full the radiator from the pond. The car started right up, and I drove the remaining two miles to the farm. A few days later I installed a new temperature sensor, a $15 item. I have rejoiced many times since then as I realized that the Holy Spirit got me through this entire 8-hour trip without an incident, and then gave me a testimony to describe and share in this book.

In the over 60 years of driving all over this great country, I have never afforded AAA coverage, and I have never had to be towed except for one accident, and that was near my daughter's home while visiting her. Transportation was readily available , of course. The Holy Spirit has always provided a solution to my car issues by getting me home or at a convenient location for the solution to be available.

Recently, I drove to my son's home in Riverview, Florida, a 45-minute drive. As I drove into the driveway and then put the gear lever in park, suddenly steam started coming from under the hood. The temperature gauge had not been showing overheating. When I opened the hood, there was a very small hose that had sprung a leak and water was spraying on the hot engine causing the steam. It was one of the most convenient parts to replace, and it took about 10 minutes after purchasing a replacement part for less than $15.

The Alero currently has a quirky starting problem. Every few days the motor will turn over but will not start. In researching the problem on the Internet, it was discovered that other people with this vintage and engine technology were also having this problem when the car is getting older. The problem is in the security system that will not let the motor start unless the electronics recognize the key as being the owner's. I experimented and determined that the problem is not the key or the ignition switch, but it is in the security computer software. The Internet describes people that are so discouraged that they junk their cars. I was able to find an expert who said that the security system could be recalibrated by turning on the key for 10 minutes while the security light blinks and then goes off. Then you must turn the key off and the engine will then start right up. However, very occasionally it will not start as there is another calibration that must vary occasionally be done that takes 15 minutes, and then starts. I stumbled on to this solution by "coincidence" (Holy Spirit) nearly a year ago, and it has never failed me. I use this calibration time to thank the Lord and to advance other's prayers.

As I am writing this chapter, I am preparing to take my beautiful Alero on a trip in a month or so, to my brother in South Carolina. I'm praying that the Holy Spirit will sanction the trip or lead me otherwise and help me prepare for the trip if I am to go with this car. In the last few days, I have had a slow leak in one of the front tires, and I took it to a garage to have it serviced. What they discovered was that it had a very small nail in an area of the tire that could not be patched but even more, they discovered "dry rot" due to the age of the tire. So, I approved two new tires be installed. Although I was not anxious to spend the money, I take it as confirmation that the Holy Spirit is guiding me in preparation for the trip. I plan on keeping the car for some time anyway, and the problem and resolution was all accomplished at or near home. Thank you, Lord!

Several years ago, I had a custom van that I had purchased for my house painting and home repair business. I had parked in a location about a mile from home, and it would not shift into gear. I called a friend, Lynn, who was a mechanical expert. When he came, he determined that there was a connection problem with the transmission. He removed the "hut" on the inside, got in the driver's seat, started the motor, reached down where the transmission was exposed, shifted it into reverse to back out of the parking space, and then forward gear to proceed home where we could repair the problem. Lynn was an angel in disguise when it came to car issues, as he had a passion for helping others and was brilliant when it came to technical issues.

Many years ago I was on a trip and was driving through Louisville, Kentucky. As we were driving down a one-way hill the electrical system shut down. We glided down the hill and into a parking slot, I noticed that we parked in front of a garage, I went into the office, it was a repair facility, they diagnosed the problem the alternator, they had a replacement, installed it and we were on the road in two hours. Hallelujah!

CHAPTER 10
THE EFFECTS OF THE HOLY SPIRIT IN US

As the son of God, Jesus has all of the powers of our Heavenly Father to communicate to us through His messenger, the Holy Spirit. Such communication can come through any of our senses such as reading scripture or other printed materials, verbally through directly speaking to us or through other people, through our mind with any manner of thoughts, or through our emotions such as love, joy and peace. He may use physical issues to communicate our health conditions and actions that He wants us to consider. He may use other people to convey messages or circumstances to teach us a lesson. He may also use the power and beauty of His creation to communicate His love and timely encouragement. He may use weather events to demonstrate His power over the circumstances that we are experiencing. And He wants us to experience the relationship and related joy of helping others in their time of need, with the resources that He provides for us to do so. And He will be with us during the storms in our life to communicate His plan, love and provision during times of trials.

He communicates to us in the inspiration that we may experience with musical talents, writing skills, athletic endeavors, as an artist, to be a motivational speaker, or any number of special skills unique to us. He may call us into the ministry to represent Him in any of a number of positions that will serve His purposes for us and for other people. And He may lead us into circumstances where we suffer difficulties and struggles, for that is when He can and will demonstrate His awareness of the details, guide us towards solutions and teaches us. We all tend to forget Him in the good times. It is in the difficult times, however, that we can seek Him and then experience Him in the details towards a resolution to these troubles.

We often sense His presence when we are "touched" by certain circumstances. This may be a compassionate moment in a movie or video, by a testimony of someone's struggles, a tender loving moment in a wedding, or a eulogy of a loved one. That being "touched" is the feeling that we have of the Holy Spirit's presence. He is saying to you "I feel your compassion, or your pain, or confirmation that He is present in your circumstance." If this being "touched" brings tears to your eyes, recognize that it is from Him and thank Him for it. That is what you want to encourage – a realization of the presence of the Holy Spirit. Why do women often cry at a wedding ceremony? They sense the power of love in the room – the unseen power of the Holy Spirit! There is a common expression that men should not cry as it shows weakness. This is absolutely wrong, for a worthy man is one that is humble and tender of heart.

The one that the Lord looks on with favor are those who are humble and contrite in spirit. (Isaiah 66:2) He honors one who has compassion and empathy for others, and the Holy Spirit can use tears to convey His presence. We can't turn them on or off by our will – only He can do it.

The effect of having the Holy Spirit in our life changes our nature and our relationship with others. That is what happens when we ask the Lord Jesus into our life, He gives us the Holy Spirit to live with us 24/7, and to help us grow to become more like how God designed us to be. The Holy Spirit is an unseen influence in our life, slowly working on our sins and shortcomings, and to help us become a better person tomorrow than we are today. The more that we realize His presence in our life, the easier it is to overcome our addictions, excesses, temptations, fears, feelings of inadequacies and attitudes. We still have to do the work of overcoming these circumstances, but the Holy Spirit is an ever-present help and encourager in these struggles.

The result of these life-altering events is for us to become more and more with a nature that brings us satisfaction, is pleasing to others and pleases Him. As that happens, the people in our life are able to see changes in us that they admire. Such specific changes are referred to in the Bible, Galatians 5:22, as fruit of the spirit. These are the attributes that are developed in our life if we are led by the Spirit:

LOVE — This is a word that is commonly understood in our society in a very limited sense, as primarily a sexual relationship. In God's world, love is unlimited in what He wants us to understand. As an example, if there was one word that defines our God, it is LOVE. In the Bible, book of John 3:16, it reads that God so loved the world that He gave His own begotten Son, that whosoever believes on Him will not perish but have everlasting life. There is no greater love than those who give up their life for others. (John 15:13) When Jesus was asked "What is the greatest commandment in the law?" He replied:"To love your God with all your heart, with all your soul, and with all your mind." (Matthew 22:36) And He said: "The second is like it, to love your neighbor as yourself." So, it is clear that the Lord God is all about love. 1 Corinthians 13:4 states that love is patient, love is kind. It does not envy, it does not boast, it is not proud. Love is not rude, it is not self-seeking, it is not easily angered. It keeps no record of wrongs. Love does not delight in evil but rejoices with the truth. It always protects, always trusts, always hopes, always perseveres. There is no direct mention of the sexual relation that we usually relate to love.

JOY — Philippians 4:4 is a directive to,"Rejoice in the Lord always. I will say it again; Rejoice!" Let your gentleness be evident to all. The Lord is near."This passage is one of the very few times in the Bible that a statement is duplicated for emphasis. The Lord Jesus often states for us not to worry: "Who, by worry can add one additional hour to your life?" (Matthew 6:25 thru 34) He makes it clear that we should not fear anything. Our fear reflects the lack of realization that He is involved and that we trust Him. Genuine joy reflects complete confidence that all will turn out OK from His viewpoint, and in the meantime, we can rejoice in His promises. We know that we need to have a positive attitude in life as it is shown to be good for our health. Laugh a lot – it is great medicine.

PEACE — Philippians 4:7 says: "Do not be anxious about anything, but in everything, by prayer and petition, present your requests to God. And the peace of God, which transcends all understanding will guard your heart and mind in Christ Jesus." I recently exercised this directive. I had several decisions to make, and my propensity is to mentally press towards a decision as soon as possible. I have come to realize that I have not been waiting for the Lord to intervene, meaning that things don't always turn out well. I now make a list of these issues, I present them to the Lord in prayer and petition, and then set them aside. As a result, I have taken my attention from them, trusting that He will lead me to a better decision at a time of His choosing. And what a peace I have as a result! I occasionally review the list, often as a reminder that I either have or have not yet received an answer, but I try my best to not mentally start processing them again. If I do dwell on an issue, especially at 5:00 in the morning, I often have to go into prayer again, reminding the Lord that I am still leaving the issue with Him, I am awaiting His answer, and in the meantime asking Him to help put me back asleep. He consistently gives me a sense of peace, and then puts me back to sleep. This morning, as I am finalizing this paragraph, the Holy Spirit put me back asleep three times between seven and eight o'clock when He consistently wakes me up.

PATIENCE — This is one of the most difficult issues that we all face. We want answers to our prayers, and we want them *now*. The Lord does not usually help resolve our issues as soon as we would like. We must realize that when we ask the Lord into our life, He is doing more than just resolving our issues – He wants us to grow into the person that He has designed us to become. Often, the answer to our concern involves other people, something that takes time for Him to orchestrate the necessary events. 2 Peter 1 describes that His power has given us everything we need, but we must demonstrate our faith in Him by exercising patience. For that faith to mature in Him, we must make every effort to add goodness, knowledge, self-control, perseverance, godliness, brotherly kindness, and love, in increasing measure.

KINDNESS — It is easy for us to be kind to those people that we love, but our Lord wants us to be kind to all people, even those who do not like us; even those who persecute us. By doing so, we radiate a specialness about our nature that may ultimately have a positive impact on them. Your reaction may eventually contribute in a positive way to spreading the love of Christ to others. In Romans 12, scripture says "If your enemy is hungry, feed him; if he is thirsty, give him something to drink. In doing this, you will heap burning coals on his head." It is the most effective way of winning over someone who has a negative attitude about you. Remember, as Jesus hung on the cross, He prayed to God: "Forgive them for they know not what they do." And very often, individual's negative attitude towards us is based on a lack of their understanding of what we are about.

GOODNESS — As Christians, by nature we want to be "good". But this fruit of the Spirit develops within us a genuine desire to help those who are in need or hurting in some way. With this attribute in us, we are willing to sacrifice some of our time and resources, not only to help someone else, but to help bring them to a closer relationship with the Lord. As a committed Christian, we should be subtly intentional in developing an empathy for others that ultimately may lead to some spiritual development in the other person.

GENTLENESS — In Isaiah 66, the Lord declares that the ones that He looks on with favor are those who are humble in spirit. Gentleness and humility relates to qualities of being kind, tender, mild-mannered, and courteous. This attribute encourages us to develop empathy, to understand and share the feelings and needs of others. This characteristic can best be illustrated by the relationship of a mother to a new-born child – a loving and gentle spirit.

SELF-CONTROL — Our choice in every aspect of life is whether we want to be in control life or do we invite the Lord to mold us into the person that He designed us to be. This is a battle inside every one of us, in every event of our life. If we want the Lord to have His way with us, we must be willing to exercise self-control over the urge to move forward on our own. By welcoming the Holy Spirit into every situation, He will help us to discipline ourselves to control our urge to "take charge and move out". We must learn to wait for the Lord to show us the resolution to our issues or we may otherwise go down a path that is contrary to His plan. What do you want: His plan or your plan? Self-control is the key to inviting Him to have His way with you, and the Holy Spirit will help you along the way.

When you seek Me you will find Me if you seek Me with all your heart.

Jeremiah 29:11

FORGIVENESS — When my wife, Katie, was with us, to the Fruits of the Spirit she would always add "forgiveness". It could be that she learned this by applying this to me – I don't know as we never discussed it. For much of my married life, I was a confident, determined husband and father, and if you had a problem just come to me and I could help fix it. I have always had an abundance of empathy – I can feel your pain. Raising my children, discipline was instilled in them (me being a West Point graduate). My philosophy was that it was my responsibility as a father to teach them "right" from "wrong." To me, everything was black and white, and don't confuse me with shades of grey. Consuming marijuana and other illegal drugs was absolutely wrong. Don't confuse me with beer and alcohol – they are OK if not consumed in excess. "As long as you are still living in my house, you will . . ." "I am not here to run a popularity campaign, I am here to teach you right from wrong, so you will do it my way as long as you eat with your feet under my table." And now, in my senior years, the Lord has shown me that I am not all knowing, that I can not change other's minds, and I certainly do not have "fixes" for others. The Lord knows what my weaknesses are and being opinionated and strong willed is something I know I have to work on. I now realize that I don't know what is best for me, let alone anyone else. What a sense of peace I get when I let Him take control of an issue that I am dealing with, but then I have to wait . . . and then wait, and then wait some more. In quiet times when I talk with Him, I try to remember that He does not need to be reminded of the issue over and over, as He never forgets. Instead, I try to thank Him as I know He will provide an answer eventually. If you continually repeat the same concern in subsequent prayers, it is basically conveying that you do not trust Him. When you lift up an issue to Him, He takes on the obligation of helping you with the need, and never forgets! Reminding Him of the same need is basically saying to Him: "In case You forgot, I ask again." And, in the meantime He will be taking care of me regarding the issue. In my meditation time, I talk to Him not in a formal way, but as a friend. This helps me to keep an open spirit, welcoming His thoughts, and intentionally taking extra time for Him without rushing off to other matters. And His thoughts are often very unique and can provide the answer, or at least guidance towards the answer.

Don't expect Him to directly resolve the issue for you, as He usually wants you to get the benefit of developing the resolution through you and not for you. In that manner, He is helping to build your confidence and trust that He "has your back". As an example, a group of us from our Sunday School Class agreed to visit a member that was in the dying phase of cancer, and the coming week she was being transferred out of state to a Catholic hospice-type of care facility for her last days. There were about 10 of us including my good friend and teacher, Ernie. We had no agenda when we went in. We started out singing Amazing Grace. Then Ernie would tell a story of something lighthearted, and then we would sing another song such as:

This world is not my home, I'm just a passing through.
My treasures are laid up somewhere beyond the blue.
The angels beckon me from heaven's open door,
and I can't feel at home in this world anymore.

Oh Lord You know I have no friend like You.
If heaven's not my home then Lord what will I do?
The angels beacon me from heaven's open door,
and I can't feel at home in this world anymore.

Song writer: Mary Reeves Davis

After that I would tell of a funny incident. Then we would sing another song, and someone would have something light-hearted to say. This went on for about 45 minutes and at times our sick friend would laugh along with us. We genuinely had a good time, we said our good-byes, and we all felt that we had been visited by the Holy Spirit.

CHAPTER 11
THEIR INCREDIBLE SPIRIT

The story I am about to relate is true and is about my hometown and church in a rural area of Ohio. The purpose of this narrative is to illustrate the common dilemma in many of our long-established churches that are currently struggling to maintain and grow a relevance in their communities. This dilemma is clearly not due to a lack of needs in the community, nor is it necessarily a lack of a spiritual calling and desire on the part of the pastors. Instead, it is apparent that it is due to the Holy Spirit not being fully understood, alive and well, by the church leadership and the parishioners. In this day and age, people are living in prosperous times with two cars in the driveway and a very nice house with all of the comforts, and they generally believe that what they have is self-earned. There is little or no appreciation that we have all received one blessing after another, and it is assumed that our prosperity will continue. The emphasis for years now is to save for the future, accumulating all that we can and invest it in growing investments. We have had it too good for so long that we do not have a basis for realizing that, compared to the rest of the world, we live like royalty. We are living in a time period and a country that has been overly blessed, and we think that we have done it on our own. Having the Lord in our lives is in head knowledge by most Christians, but few understand and embrace the realization that the Holy Spirit has been the driving force in developing this great country since its inception and providing all of our goodies. And, if practicing Christians do not know and appreciate the involvement of the Holy Spirit, the community at large doesn't have a clue.

This story is an attempt to illustrate what our ancestors appreciated in their lives, beginning in the year 1880 in this little town in northwest Ohio. The town consisted of about 600 people with surrounding farmland made up of hardy, hardworking people primarily from Europe, many from Germany, and from Britain. They were extremely grateful people, fleeing from the oppression of opportunities and thrilled with the possibilities of ownership of their own homes, businesses and freedom to worship. The town was home to small business owners, educators and trade workers. The farmers in the area were carving out their farms by diking and draining very fertile land from the Black Swamp and claiming the land from dense woodlands and underbrush. Electricity, cars, trucks and tractors had not yet been invented, so everything was done by hand without power equipment of any kind. A Methodist church had been organized many years before, starting in a one-room school until a wood-frame worship center was constructed. This building was soon found to be too small, and fire was a common concern, so a brick one was built in 1869.

About 10 years later, May of 1880, the night was punctuated by a great deal of commotion. The business part of town was on fire, and a very strong wind was aggressively spreading the fire. There was no effective fire department that could tame it , and it finally burned itself out. A total of over 35 structures were either destroyed or badly damaged including the church, where only the bell from the tower and the pulpit were saved. (Figure10-1) Many of the business families lived above their businesses and, fortunately, there was no loss of life. Only a few of the destroyed buildings were insured. An investigation into the cause eventually revealed that a gang of arsonists were paid by a property owner to obtain an insurance settlement.

The church congregation was an extremely spirited people in those days, greatly thankful to the Lord for the blessings that they were enjoying despite the hardships here in the land of the free and the home of the brave. The congregation was so passionate for having a sanctuary that the same year as the fire, a brick replacement was constructed, including a sizable bell tower. (Figure 10-2) The congregation was growing so fast, that a larger and more ornate tribute to the Lord was then designed and built. This beautiful sanctuary was dedicated in 1906 which stands today as a testimony to the enlivened spirit of the people of those days. (Figure 10-3).

And now it is over 100 years later, and this church stands boldly and beautifully – a remarkable structure reflecting the enormous spirit of those people of the time. They were determined to build a sanctuary that reflected their love and gratitude to the Lord, demonstrating their devotion, determination and willing sacrifice. The worship area seats between 250 and 300 people. Balconies were built for overflow worshipers. This Methodist denomination was well known for Bible studies and Sunday School classes, so classrooms were included on both the first and second floor. A choir loft was included that would hold up to 30 singers. A full basement was included with a large dining area and kitchen to accommodate monthly covered-dish dinners and special occasions.

In the sanctuary a beautiful stain-glass window was included that is approximately 25 feet high, depicting the baby Jesus, Mother Mary, Joseph and a donkey (Figure 8-4) – all of which radiates love for Jesus' birth. Arched decorative windows surround this greatly inspired depiction that are ornate and hovered over by two angels. The framework was made from solid hardwood that hold these windows in place, made by hand without power tools of any kind. It is apparent that cost reduction was not a consideration since the sanctuary includes a second window of equal size and stain-glass windows are in every room on both the first and second floor, for a total of 30 windows. Considering the time period, where could these windows have come from? Where were they inspired, how could they have been shipped, erected and framed with such care that now, over 100 years later, they have stood the test of time and still look as perfect as when new?

About 40 feet above the worship area is a beautiful large dome accommodating a stain-glass window in the center. As a reminder, 40 feet is the equivalent of a four-story building. This circular dome was made using strips of wood (lath) and plaster. It is as perfectly shaped and as beautiful today as ever!

The pews in the main part of the sanctuary are made from solid hardwood without a hint of a knot. These pews are not straight on, they are curved around the sanctuary. They are extremely heavy, the ends of which are ornately carved. How could they be cut and shaped by hand from trees with such perfection that they are as beautiful and solid today as when new? This beautiful sanctuary was dedicated in 1906 and participation at the ceremony is shown in Figure 10-5. What an inspiration this building is and a loud proclamation by our forefathers as to their passionate love and appreciation to the Lord!

And where are we today? When this chapter is being written in late September, vacations are over, the children are back to school, and the town population has grown to about 1,200. Attendance at church is averaging about a dozen children and less than 15 adults in Sunday School, with worship attendance about 80. A Family Life Center building was built across the street from the church a few years ago. This is a very nice, functional building of modern design and financed with a 20-year loan. There are no stain glass windows and nothing ornate. What is the difference between then and now? What is missing? The economy is by far the best it has ever been, businesses are begging for employees, children are from families with divorce rates skyrocketing and suicide rates never having been this high before. In addition, our society is politically polarized with anger abounding.

I am hereby staking a claim that the Holy Spirit is little understood, especially in our Christian communities! As citizens of this great country, we lack appreciation for how blessed we are *by Him*, and how grateful we should be for being blessed so abundantly here in America! His Holy Spirit needs to be learned about and welcomed enthusiastically individually, in this community and to this country – the last bastion of freedom of expression and worship in the world! We need a revival, but it needs to start with us individually, with a passion to embrace the Holy Spirit in every moment, every thought, every word and every action of every day. We need to realize that He gives us this gift not just to help us in our walk with Him, but to have a burning desire to help other people find the Living Lord in their life as well. May our passion for the Holy Spirit become as strong as it obviously was in our early ancestors!

CHAPTER 12
MY BROTHER NEIL

On September 8, 1938 my brother Neil was born the third of five boys in our family. In a few weeks it became evident that he had developmental issues. He was a slow learner and it was thought that he may have had a slight case of polio as an infant, an illness that was beginning to show up in people in those days. Although this illness could not be confirmed, he was slow at learning to walk, talk or express himself and coordination development was also slow to come. In time he did learn to walk, talk and express himself, although haltingly. He did not have enough coordination to catch a ball which what all we boys did for recreation. As he became older, he began school along with others his age. His nature was to be happy with himself and was not frustrated with his condition. When he became a teenager, we were all convinced that he would not graduate from high school, would never learn to drive a car, and probably not be able to hold down a job. Certainly, Neil would never be married and have a family. Our parents were always extremely concerned about who would look after him when they were gone.

As he grew up, my parents were always loving and patient with him. When he was a year old, they would take him once a month for physical therapy to help him develop coordination in his right arm. In those days, to be left-handed was considered a handicap to be avoided and Neil's right arm was under-developed. For that reason, my parents took him to a chiropractor once a month for several years for the therapist to work with his arm. As time went by, this proved to be extremely beneficial, as he became right- handed and his arm developed normally.

My parents were faithful church attenders, always participating in Sunday School and all church events such as Lenten Holy Week and Christmas Advent services. My father enjoyed singing in the men's choir at the monthly county-wide Methodist Church gatherings and when I was a teen, he would invite me to sing with him. My mother was noted to have the best baked-bean casserole at the church monthly family covered-dish dinners that we always attended. Neil loved to go to church and was faithful in his attendance at the weekly Sunday School classes and summer Vacation Bible School events.

As time went by, he ended up graduating with his high school class, having been carried through with the rest of the class. He not only obtained his drivers license but in his first job working for a farmer's grain and feed company, he was able to back up customer's trailers to the loading platform if they wanted his help. He worked there until the business closed and then was hired at the Fayette Tubular Company where he worked for the next 35 years. He enjoyed his work, always showing up 20 to 30 minutes early and diligently working his best despite the fact that he was doing the most undesirable job in the company – degreasing parts that had oil and grease that needed cleaning.

It was reported that Neil was so dedicated to his work that when the Corporate CEO visited the plant to talk with employees, after a few minutes of conversation, Neil politely excused himself as he had work to do. When the plant was closed, Neil's seniority number was #3 out of nearly 200 employees.

During Neil's employment at Fayette Tubular he met and dated a lady about his age, and a few years later they were married. Neil was 48 years old at the time. Our parents were elated as they were always concerned about who would care for him in his older years, and they really loved Ila, his wife. Within a year after they were married, Ila was informed by the State of Ohio Human Services that her three grandchildren were in foster care due to the poor conditions they were found living in with their parents. The oldest child was 8 and the twin boys were 2 years old. Neil and Ila willingly adopted them, and suddenly Neil had a family of his own. Soon after, they decided to move to a rustic family cottage in the upper part of Michigan, about 300 miles away, where they could start over and get away from the scrutiny of the small town. Neil had inherited the cottage. Neil was by nature, a pleasant, humble and loving person who knew right from wrong, and proceeded to be the steady, caring male figure that the family needed and had never known before. Neil was a reliable income earner and when his wife became ill, he willingly took over as a loving husband and father for them all. He would get the boys up in the morning for school, always fed them breakfast and was there for them at the end of the school day. He did the shopping for groceries and the cooking. He volunteered at school whenever they could use him, and the teachers would remark about how cooperative the kids were. Neil was clear about the attitudes expected of the boys, and they adored him and were never a discipline problem. When the children went to bed, Neil would read to them and taught them to pray. Neil and his wife enjoyed driving excursions, and even took a trip to Nashville to see the Grand Ole Opry.

By the time Neil's wife died, Cody, the oldest grandson, was in his late 20's and recently married. The twins were ready to graduate from high school. When Ila died Neil's three remaining brothers had decisions to make as to where Neil could best live out his remaining years. For various reasons, none of us were in a position to provide for his care. In a short while, Cody came to us and said that he and his recently-married wife would really like Neil to move in with them, and they would take care of him for the rest of his life. Cody said that they all really loved Neil and greatly appreciated what he had done for them. As a result, Neil lived with them for the next eight years of his life during which he helped raise two great-grandchildren. Because of Neil's soft-spoken and loving spirit the children were naturally attracted to him. When Neil died, these last two children were significantly affected by his loss.

At Neil's Celebration of Life ceremony, it was apparent that all who knew him loved and respected him. Upon reflection, it became evident that, despite his disability and the low expectations we all had for him in his early years, the Lord had great plans for him. It was recognized at the Celebration that as his life played out, Neil never worried about his future and was never anxious over his circumstances. This is what the Lord wants for all of us – to be the great shepherd leading us and encouraging us to allow His plan to be played out unhindered by our expectations. The Lord wants us to live with total faith and trust in Him. Neil was a great testimony to such a life, as every concern that we had for him was resolved by our Loving Father through the Holy Spirit.

CHAPTER 13

KAREN'S WALK WITH THE HOLY SPIRIT

By Karen McDonnald

God did not give us a spirit of timidity, but a spirit of power, of love, and of self-discipline.
1 Timothy 1:7

I want to acknowledge my mother, and in this writing I want to talk about her unwavering faith. She provided loving parental guidance and a witness for me to aspire to. She was of Italian descent. As a young person, I know there were a lot of Italian jokes about how determined the women were; one that comes to mind is the cartoon of a skeleton sitting on the park bench. The caption reads: "Me waiting for an Italian girl to apologize." I know in relation to the word of God, this attitude would be one of being stubborn and prideful, to name a few. But as I look back at the women in our family it was their strength and faith that kept us all together. (Plus, a little attitude of . . . "I'm gonna make you an offer you can't refuse")

When my mother set her sight on something, if she were to have her own personal dictionary, I know for a fact that words like "unbelief, doubt, can't", would not be included. I think God gave her a double portion of faith and patience. I remember arguments or disagreements with her, but I never stood a chance. When I think of the scripture "if you will say to the mountain be thou removed and cast into the sea. . .", that might work on anyone else in the world but not on her as she knew of that scripture long before I ever did. She was determined that I was going to be the mountain that was going to be removed, not her.

As an example, when I was younger my father worked for General Motors and had lost his job through some unfortunate circumstances. But it was my mom who got dressed like the professional woman that she was when she meant business – bouffant hair-do and all. Again, with her God faith and confidence, she marched herself into his office and spoke to whomever the Lord led her to speak to, and his job was restored.

My aunts and my grandmother were the same. They were Christian women who knew if they stood on their faith, with the Lord's help anything was possible. They have all passed away except for my Aunt Marie that I consider my second mother after my mother passed away. Even though she is 84 at this time, she is still to this day as strong if not stronger in her walk with the Lord. I believe that if Jesus were here today, He would say of her as he did the centurion: "I have not found such great faith, not even in Israel." (Matthew 8:10)

Your love, oh Lord, reaches to the heavens
Your faithfulness stretches to the sky
Your righteousness is like the mighty mountains
Your justice flows like the ocean's tide.

I will lift my voice to worship You, my King
I will find my strength in the shadow of Your wings.

Song by Third Day

Around 18 years ago, I had made the commitment to the Lord that I would never make another major decision without seeking Him in prayer first. Of course, I didn't realize that also meant waiting on Him for an answer. (I'm a slow learner – thankfully the Lord provides an abundance of grace and mercy). It wasn't until 2 years ago that my life took a turn on a profound direction that I had never thought possible. I had been praying for a closer walk with the Lord and little did I know that I was about to embark on just that.

In the past when I would have problems or concerns about things going on in my life, I would always go to the Lord in prayer. Many times, not every time, I would get a glimpse of what the answer would be or at least some idea of what direction I was to go. However, these past two years I have not perceived in my spirit the answer to my major problem. This has baffled me, especially since I can usually stand in prayer with others and they might receive an answer or pertinent advice. I do believe that the Lord has provided some clues to my dilemma, but I will not know until the answer manifests itself. Hopefully, it will be in the near future and not the far one – and I will share more on this subject as events unfold.

As I mentioned, I had been praying for a closer walk with the Lord and these past two years have provided just that. Little did I know, I would not continue on the road I was on (for the time being) but began a different journey with Him. At first, I started out with bitter weeping, excruciating emotional pain, and hopelessness. Little by little, however, my walk evolved into a more spiritual walk with Him opening my eyes to understanding what it is like to walk only by faith. Faith is all that I had left when I couldn't see any kind of sign of hope in this earthly realm. At first, I had to get over the shock of what had happened, and then I started to settle in and know in my spirit that I would be spending more time with the Lord and less and less time with friends and family. I have been blessed to be able to spend most of my days with Him, meditating on His word, and most of all learning to walk by faith and not by sight. This, by the way, has taken me almost two years to learn. During this time the Lord has been trying to teach me that no longer will He lead me the way that He has in the past.

As a result, the first significant lesson began with scripture … "I walk by faith and not be sight" (2 Corinthians 5:7) and I could recall many other scriptures about faith. I truly believed that I walked wholeheartedly by faith before, but the Lord showed me that there's more to it than just believing that you can.

As the days came and went, I realized that I was spending more and more quality time with the Lord. My eyes of understanding were opened about healing, and other scripture seemed to make more sense to me. However, there was still a certain amount of frustration because I was not receiving from Him the answer that I most desired. I would ask, seek, knock (Matthew 7:7) and would hear nothing. I would even add in some tears and pleading, and I would even try to reason with the Lord. At one point even, I got a bit of an "attitude". Trust me I quickly repented as I realized that to be upset with Him was a very foolish thing to do. When my one granddaughter turned 13, I got to spend a couple days with her alone. I told her my frustration with not hearing from the Lord the way that I thought He should answer. She just smiled at me and said, "The Lord is giving you the answer; He is telling you to wait." I just sighed and told her "I don't know how you got to be so smart – I think you are absolutely right!" By the way she has the prettiest smile and I don't even have the words to express how sweet her spirit is. She obviously has the Holy Spirit in her life. After her statement, I had to continuously remind myself that the Lord's timing is always perfect, and He often communicates wisdom through the spirit of a child. That was almost a year ago now, and I am still waiting for my "answer". However, I recently was reminded in a sermon message … "in due time …" Ding, ding, ding! The Holy Spirit is saying that He hasn't forgotten. and the answer is still coming. I knew then that my answer could come "in due time" and the lesson is to stand in complete faith.

I continue to struggle for an answer and at times I am tired of feeling like I am defeated, but I am determined to overcome this darkness no matter how long it takes. I am standing on scripture, but now it has become my mission in life to trust the Lord with all my heart and lean not on my own understanding. (Proverbs 3:5). I also have learned that doubt and unbelief try to sneak in, but I stand firm every day, and cast those thought down. Ephesians 6 talks about the Armor of God and verse 16 states that *above all else* to take up the shield of faith with which you can extinguish all the flaming arrows of the evil one. Notice that it tells us *above all else*, and this is the way I think of it; *faith* is a *force* that surrounds me at all times. I look at it as a shield that can be moved in every direction to protect me, So, everyday my faith gets stronger and stronger if I do my part by using my shield of faith when *the evil one* starts firing darts in my thoughts. That is the time I declare out loud in a prayer for Satan to depart in the name of Jesus, and he does! That is my shield of faith – the Lord wants me to do the fighting against Satan and He gives me the power to do so in His name! This is the lesson that I need to continue to remind myself *at all times* when I have worries or concerns. As a believer in Him I have the power and authority to fight the darkness in my life. In 1 John 1:5-7 it states that in Him there is no darkness at all and if we claim to have fellowship with him but allow darkness to enter into our life, *we lie* and do not live in the truth. Therefore, I have learned that if I allow darkness into my thoughts, it is a sin, and I have the power to pray it away – in the name of Jesus.

As a result, for the first time in my life I feel *free*! I feel like whatever battle comes my way, I can stand in faith and watch the Lord do His part and get the victory! I believe the word when it tells me "He'll never test us beyond what we can bear" (1 Corinthians 10:13). So, I know when I'm faced with a problem, He already has the answer. I believe that he has provided me with faith and patience to help me endure the challenges in my life while He works his plan for a resolution. Jesus also tells us to cast all our cares on Him and leave it with Him (1 Peter 5:7). I can testify that He has been faithful and just and can win any battle if I just give it to Him with complete faith. I am totally convinced that He has put everything in place for me to walk with Him through all the challenges in my life that I will be facing in the future, and that He is waiting on the other side with me to declare victory.

Victory in Jesus

I heard an old, old story, how a Savior came from glory,
How He gave His life on Calvary to save a wretch like me:
I heard about His groaning, of His precious blood's atoning,
Then I repented of my sins and won the victory.

I heard about His healing, of His cleansing power revealing:
How He made the lame to walk again and caused the blind to see,
and then I cried, "Dear Jesus, come and heal my broken spirit,"
and somehow Jesus came and brought to me the victory.

I heard about a mansion He has built for me in glory,
And I heard about the streets of gold beyond the crystal sea,
about the angels singing, and the old redemption story,
and some sweet day I'll sing up there the song of victory.

O victory in Jesus, my Savior forever,
He sought me and bought me with His redeeming blood.
He loved ere I knew him, and all my love is due Him,
He plunged me to victory, beneath the cleaning flood.

In 2004 living in Florida, we had several hurricanes that came through the state. I was living in a small mobile home. It was so small that if it would've had a hitch at one end, I could've pulled it with a pickup truck. Now, of course, it seems to be the new craze with the "tiny house movement."

If you live in or are familiar with the tropics you know that the month of June means a lot of heat and humidity, rain, and fun in the sun if you can somehow avoid having a heat stroke. I have very little tolerance to the heat anymore. I really thought something was seriously wrong with me until I learned my doctor suffers the same thing. He told me that he goes from his home, to the car, to the next building that has an abundance of air conditioning. I was glad to hear that I was not alone with this issue.

Early summer in Florida begins the season for hurricanes, and it was around the start of the season in 2004, that I had a dream. In my dream I saw the aftermath of a hurricane all around my home, with acres of huge grandfather oaks uprooted and snapped in two like toothpicks. Power lines were down, fallen trees and debris everywhere. But in my dream my little mobile home was still standing, unharmed. Little did I know that two months later, my dream would come to pass.

It was mid-August and trouble was brewing in the Caribbean. The first thing that I did when I heard about it was to go to the Lord in prayer and declared that I was going to stand in complete faith that He would be with me and protect me if the hurricane came my way. The next thing that I did was to get a few non-perishables, batteries and extra water. I did have access to a sturdy building that was only about 100 feet away, so my plan was to go there and wait the storm out.

In the morning of the arrival of the hurricane, around 5 am, the winds were picking up along with heavy rain, and I heard a very loud noise outside nearby. I then heard it again a few minutes later. I couldn't see outside as it was still dark, and all that I could do was wait for sunrise. As you can imagine, I was deep in prayer! When I could see, the grandfather oaks nearby were snapped in two like toothpicks. A short time later, I made my way to the building and waited until the storm let up before returning home. Once it was safe to survey the damage, I found that only a small piece of my awning had blown off and otherwise my mobile home was intact. As I looked beyond my yard by a few hundred feet, I could see oak trees snapped in two, and power poles down and transformers blown. As I drove around the neighborhood, I saw the devastation that the Lord had shown me only a few months prior in my dream, but I was safe, and my home protected from any damage!

God's way is perfect. All the Lord's promises prove true.
He is a shield for all who look to Him for protection.

CHAPTER 14

MORE OF KAREN'S WALK WITH THE HOLY SPIRIT

By Karen McDonnald

A few years ago, I went through some things in my life that were, to say the least, devastating. The past 15 years prior to that, I had committed my life wholeheartedly to the Lord, but scripture tells us, "In this life you will have trials and tribulations." (John 16:33). I found myself in a "whirlwind" that left me dumbfounded and asking the Lord, "How could this happen and why?" What I want to share in this testimony is what I experienced from the Lord that I had never experienced before and that was *His Perfect Peace!*

During this time of tribulation, I would cry every day and it would get to the point that my heart would start to race. and I would feel like my air supply was being cut off. I would tell myself, or should I say the enemy would say to me "…you're not gonna make it! You're probably gonna have a stroke or something and you're probably gonna need some real good medication to get through this!" But one day as I was experiencing such a depression, a peace suddenly came over me with a sense that everything would be OK. This was a peace beyond all understanding! (Philippians 4:7). The first time it happened I don't remember thinking much about it at the time. But then it happened a second and then a third time. By then it left me in a state of calm, and I knew it was the Lord's peace and comfort that I was experiencing.

It wasn't long after that that the Lord showed me the scripture, John 14:26:

> "But the Counselor, the Holy Spirit, whom the Father will send in My name, will teach you all things and will remind you of everything I have said to you. Peace I leave with you, My peace I give you. I do not give to you as the world gives. Do not let your heart be troubled and do not be afraid."

I had previously never experienced His gift of peace, and it went to my heart, mind and soul like never before! His peace was so pure that I could not help but embrace it. It was so profound that I felt His peace flowing through me and left me with bewilderment as to what just happened. I felt assurance that in His time everything would work out

When I think of my life before this event, if I was asked to define the word "peace", it would be when things are quiet and going just fine, healthy, and nothing is "broken". This is what Jesus described as "Peace the world gives." But my "life crisis" changed everything. I couldn't begin to imagine how this happened - how can He infuse such a sense of assurance, a kind of love compassion into me? During my scripture readings, I believe that Jesus gave me a clue in John 15:4, "Abide in me, and I in you. As the branch cannot bear fruit of itself, unless it abides in the vine, neither can you, unless you abide in

Me." I learned that when I fully believed in Him, His sacrifice on the cross and resurrection, He abides in me and His peace flows in like a gentle river. This is the unseen world that I was experiencing as identified in Ephesians 6:12, "Our struggle is not against flesh and blood, but against the rulers, against the powers of this dark world and against the spiritual forces of evil in the heavenly realms." So, I now realize that my "spiritual warfare" is in my mind and in my being, and I am given the power and authority, in the name of Jesus, to win every such struggle. I discovered in the book of Luke verses 10:16-18, Jesus said "You have been given authority over all the power of the enemy and you can walk among snakes and scorpions and crush them. Nothing will injure you. But you are not to rejoice because evil spirits obey you, rejoice because your names are registered in heaven."

One of my favorite healing testimonies is about one of my granddaughters, Addison, who was staying with me for a few days. It was Easter 2018 and after church we made our way to the Cracker Barrel restaurant to meet my daughter and other three granddaughters that we had not seen for some time. Addison and I arrived before the others and we felt very hungry as we had not eaten breakfast. After an hour of waiting they called our name and we were seated. Our waitress promptly asked to take our drink order, and Addison requested a Coke. I thought that it would be OK – how was I to know that Coke on an empty stomach of a 7 year- old would spell disaster? Finally, our other family members arrived and what a joy to have an Easter meal with them. Addison had talked non-stop with excitement since learning of their coming. After drinking some of the Coke, I knew something was going on when she started getting quiet, then wanted to set next to me and put her head in my lap. I noticed that she started getting chill bumps on her arms, then the tears started. She said that her stomach was hurting, and I needed to take her to the bathroom. She told me that she thought she was going to get sick and did I have any peppermint essential oil that might help her. Her mother is a walking encyclopedia when it comes to oils and natural remedies, and Addison is following in her mother's footsteps in that regard. I believe in them too and usually I carry several oils with me, but not that day. When I told her that I didn't, she asked me to take her home. I knew that she was not playing games with me as she had been so excited to see her cousins. After we got our order to go, I rushed her out to the car. I prayed that we could get home before she got sick to her stomach, but I might have to pull over to the side of the road a time or two as we had nearly an hour's drive home. I got her settled in the back seat and had her lie down and rest.

Now, I had recently heard a teaching on healing, speaking to our sickness and commanding it in the name of Jesus to leave. I had tried this on myself and others several times, and it *really worked!* So, after getting her buckled in, I got in the driver's seat, started the car, and as I was beginning to leave the parking lot the Holy Spirit spoke these words to me: "Pray for her." I pulled over and told Addison that I'm going to pray for her. In her sweet voice she said OK. So, I started out "In the name of Jesus

..." and she repeated it. "...I command that the stomach pains leave her body, because by the stripes of Jesus she *is healed* – we believe it and receive it in Jesus name." Addison had continued to pray every word with me. I again suggested that she try to take a nap and I would get her home as soon as I could. Amazingly, by the time we got out of the parking lot she said: "MeMaw I feel better!" (That's what my grandkids call me.) I said:"That's wonderful – Hallelujah!" and she ended up napping all the way home and exclaimed that she felt good!

I get goose bumps every time that I tell this story, and it reminds me of the scripture where Jesus could only heal a handful of people because of their lack of faith. I believe that children that love us trust us and believe what we tell them. Jesus has told us to have a child-like faith. Addison had no reason to doubt, and that is why healing came.

> He was wounded for our transgressions, He was bruised for our
> inequities; the chastisement for our peace was upon Him, and by
> His stripes we are healed.

> Isaiah 53:5

Jesus has given us the power and authority to heal the sick (Mark 16:18). Recently my dear cousin, Linda, fell and broke her ankle. We prayed together and believed that she would be healed. But at one point after she came home from the hospital and was slowly on the mend, she felt that she had the start of an infection where they had put in screws and plates. She then saw a wound care specialist and he confirmed that the site was not healing like it should. She and her husband were both convinced that things were going from bad to worse. After several days of concern, she called me, and we discussed what the specialist had told her. I need to mention that Linda is a "mighty prayer warrior". At any time when I am on the phone with her, if she even has the slightest inclination from the Holy Spirit that something is amuck in my life, she breaks out in a mighty spiritual warfare prayer as her Spirit leads her. Most of the time she is the one praying and interceding for our family, but at that time she was the one needing prayer. After listening to her intersession for so many years, I then realized that it was my turn to be bold. I then started praying, commanding any infection in that area to be gone in Jesus' name. We both took a stand on the scripture that says, "by the stripes of Jesus she is healed." We believed it and she would receive it and we're thanking the Lord for her healing, praising Him, and we laughed and carried on. Suddenly the Holy Spirit inside of me came alive. I had never felt anything like this before. I stopped laughing and I told her ... "Linda, you're healed!" I told her a second time that she was healed, and we continued to thank the Lord and to praise Him. We knew that Satan walks about like a roaring lion seeking who he may devour (1 Peter 5:8). Scripture tells us that he comes to steal, kill and destroy (John 10:10). Although doubt tended to come to us, we continued to walk in faith that she was healed. Understand that she had been stuck at home in a wheelchair, unable to walk for four months. When she went back to the hospital, the ER doctor and surgeon both confirmed she was healed of the injury and there was no sign of infection. Thank you, Lord!

Once I learned that I was able to rebuke, command and take authority over the enemy in my life, especially when it came to healing, (physical, mental and emotionally), I felt liberated! As a result, gone are the days of complaining of a headache, nausea, backache, etc. I learned that I can rebuke these things and command them to leave my body *in the name of Jesus*. I then stand on healing scriptures such as: *By the stripes of Jesus I will be healed!* And if I was healed at that time, I would declare . . . *I was healed* or *I am healed, hallelujah*!! I then say, "*I believe it and I receive it in Jesus name!*" I then stand in complete faith that I am healed. I verbalize that that I no longer give the enemy a place of glory by speaking that I'm sick. Sometimes Satan can try to convince me that I have one thing after another going on – I speak from experience here – but I reject the thoughts.

Even on an emotional level the enemy speaks lies if we let him. He has tried to keep me in a constant state of feeling defeated and living in a vicious cycle of depression, but I have learned to identify that he is a liar and a thief and I demand that he leave! *Sickness is not from God!* It is under the curse – review Isaiah 53:4-5 and see that Jesus took away all of it over 2000 years ago if we just believe it!

The other thing that I now pay more attention to are the words that I speak. They are just words and I can either speak life or death. Psalm 18:21 says that Life and Death is in the power of the tongue, and those who love it will eat its fruit. Galatians 6:7 tells us that we will reap whatever we sow. This is a principle of both the spiritual and the natural worlds. Our words have power, so whatever we speak and stand in faith on is what will come to pass.

Another thing that I want to share is that one evening the Lord spoke to me in my spirit, and said *people are so quick to believe Satan's lies over My truths*. In thinking about it, when someone tells me *that's never going to happen* or *You're not capable of doing that* I don't believe it – I rebuke it in the name of Jesus! His name is above every name in heaven and on earth – His name is above any sickness and disease – His name is above My financial disaster, my marriage, my job or whatever it is that I'm going through. I know who I am in Christ and *believe in His word!* His word tells me that I am the apple of His eye. *I believe it!!* The word tells me that I am more than a conqueror, *and I believe it!!* I believe what the word says when it says to get rid of anything that is under the curse.

When these truths really sank in and took root in my heart and in my spirit, it completely changed my life. I can honestly say that I believe that *I can do all things through Christ who strengthens me!* And *I am more than a conqueror!* The other scripture that I started listening to is *Cast all your cares on Him because He cares for you!* When I really started doing this, not only did I give it to the Lord and leave it with Him, I know with all of my heart that He has the answers and His answers are much better than anything I could come up with. What a load of worry it takes off my shoulders and is replaced by a sense of peace!

I believe that we are living in the last days and I am seeing more manifestations of the Lord. (According to the prophet Joel 2:28-32). Therefore, it is time to be bold in the faith and proclaim His goodness to all who will believe.

CHAPTER 15
TRIP TO SOUTH CAROLINA

By Dean Bates

This chapter will focus on more of the daily-type experiences, not the more dramatic, where the Holy Spirit is involved in all details of a recent trip last year to my brother and his wife in South Carolina. Unless we develop a sensitivity for the Spirit, he is often very subtle in his influence in the events of our life and we tend to not recognize and appreciate His involvement.

For the past several years my brother, Lyle, has been caring for his wife who has been declining in health with Alzheimer's. He has been totally dedicated to caring for her the rest of her life, if possible. I have found in the past that when I visit, they are both stimulated by the freshness of our conversations. After spending four months in Ohio last year, as I returned to Florida I called to see when the best time would be for me to drive up for a visit. Lyle suggested that I come to attend a wonderful musical Christmas event at the Baptist Church where their daughter and husband actively participate. On Friday before I planned to depart on Monday, during the first part of December, Lyle called and announced that he had to agree to take Marilyn to a care facility. Her knees had collapsed and fell, fortunately without breaking anything, but he was unable to get her up without a neighbor's help. Also, she had been unable to cooperate with him dressing, eating, and basic functioning for some time. He had no choice but to enroll her into a care facility. I said that I would be coming as planned for the Christmas program at the church.

It had now been over four years since the Lord took my dear wife, Katie, home and I have stayed positive and enthusiastic every day as I was aware that the Lord had a plan for me each and everyday of my remaining life. However, I have a residual loneliness that I continue to struggle with every single day. This comes on about five o'clock in the afternoon as the day's activities wind down, and especially on Sunday afternoons. Spare time seems to be my enemy! To help cope, I typically bicycle ride six miles every day through my neighborhoods, and on Sunday I ride 10 miles. In this way, I stay fit and at the same time enjoy the Florida climate while taking up spare time. Just a few days before the trip to South Carolina, in my daily bible study I came across this scripture from 1 John 1:5-7.

"This is the message we have heard from Him and declare to you: God is light; in Him there is no darkness at all. If we claim to have fellowship with Him and yet walk in the darkness, *we lie* and do not live out the truth. But if we walk in the light, we have fellowship with one another, and the blood of Jesus, his Son, purifies us from all sin."

This convinced me that although nearly all of my time during the day is consciously walking in the light with Him, staying positive, I am letting darkness (loneliness)in my life. This is the result of a lack of fully trusting in His awareness and plans to resolve this issue in His time and in His way. I never intentionally want to "lie", but I have been claiming that I have fellowship with Him and yet I am letting darkness in my life. This became a very clear realization that the Holy Spirit knows all about this struggle and I need to fully trust Him!

And now back to my journey up to South Carolina, and I departed the following Wednesday. During the trip I dedicated the time to focusing on the Lord and becoming more sensitive to examples of how the Holy Spirit is present in the details of this journey. I specifically asked the Lord to fill this trip up with examples that I may use in this book as testimonies of the Holy Spirit.

During this ten-hour trip, I listened to some Christian music, and three songs really spoke to me:

- Maybe it's Time to Let the Old Ways Die

- Don't Worry, Be Happy

- How Long Has It Been Since You've Been on Your Knees?

When I arrived at my brother's house, I learned that Marilyn had already been admitted two days before into a very nice care facility. This facility is where Lyle and Marilyn had, for several years before, conducted a sing-along ministry with Marilyn playing the piano. For them it was like returning to some old friends. The previous day, the first full day that she was there, she did not know Lyle and didn't have energy enough to even get out of bed. On Friday, when Lyle and I visited, she was in a wheelchair with a group of others in a gathering place near her room. Although she could not talk, it was apparent that she recognized us. We wheeled her to the activities room that had a piano for me to play. I played several songs, and she was energized enough to move to the beat while sitting in her wheelchair. Lyle asked her if she would like to dance, and she motioned that she would, and he helped her up and they danced to my music.

The following Sunday afternoon was the Christmas program that I had originally came to South Carolina to attend. This turned out to be the most amazing musical event that I have ever attended *in my life*! It was called Keyboards & Carols at the First Baptist Church in Spartanburg. There were a total of six grand pianos, four keyboards and the church's beautiful old pipe organ. The program featured a variety of these instruments playing together as well as separately, all with unique orchestrations composed just for the occasion. It was so beautiful that it was breathtaking.

Each day, we would visit Marilyn and push her in her wheelchair to the entertainment room for my musical time, just with her and Lyle. One afternoon as we were going home, I mentioned to the facility director that I would be back the next afternoon for another piano concert, and if they would like to bring other residents in, they might also enjoy the music. When I came the next day, there were about 40 people already waiting for me to play. Between numbers, I would talk with them about inspirational matters, such as how the Lord had a plan for them every day, to do what He would inspire them to do. As an example, they could reach out to someone that they did not know and make a friend – everyone can use another friend. To eat at a different table occasionally to show your interest in others. To make phone calls and be an encouragement to others that need a friend checking on them.

On Sunday after church our entire family gathered for a lunch at Lyle's son and daughter-in-law's home, Randy and Maria, along with two grandkids, a husband and a son. It is traditional that they have lunch together and then play a card game after church on Sunday. . A good time was had by all, and no one was in a hurry to leave. Late in the afternoon, we all went to visit Marilyn and had one more sing-along together as a family.

The next day, Monday, Lyle invited me to go with him to watch his grandson play soccer at a nearby sports center. This facility turned out to be the most beautiful, extensive sports facility in the southeast part of the United States. It was built by The First Baptist Church of Spartanburg, and it is a first-class facility in every way, for both indoor and outdoor sports. It is called "Upward Star Center, and has multiple basketball and volleyball courts, a fitness center, a cafeteria, and indoor facilities for activities such as cheerleading. All practices and activities are begun with a bible teaching time, and Christ is proclaimed throughout. Outdoor facilities include baseball, softball, soccer, lacrosse, and flag football as well as batting cages and pitching tunnels. It is busy every day, packed with activities, summer and winter.

On Tuesday, Lyle and I visited a neighborhood friend and his wife, Jimmie and Jane Farmer. I met them and toured their house, a beautiful, restored southern home. He is a retired pastor, and their story of the Lord in their lives was so fascinating that I invited them to write it out as their testimony, and it is included in this book.

On Wednesday, I returned to Tampa all the while thanking the Lord for answering my appeal to Him to fill this trip with examples of where the Holy Spirit was present. Considering that the only event that I had planned was to attend the Christmas Program, the entire time was filled – every day—with the presence of the Holy Spirit in significant ways!

CHAPTER 16

PASTOR JIMMIE'S TESTIMO-NY

By Jimmie and Jane Farmer

Every high school graduate is always asked the same question – what do you want to do with your life? Many graduates have a career in mind that often means getting a college degree, and this is usually encouraged by family and friends. Many don't know what they want to do, but decide to go to college anyway. Some want to go in the military, and some just want to stay at home and develop a skill learning a trade. Some just don't know and just get some kind of a job. The graduates with the most uncertain path are those who have received a calling from the Lord to minister to others, so they enroll in seminary and let the Lord lead them on the path the Lord wants them to journey, one day at a time. Such as it was for me, as I felt the Holy Spirit prompt me to attend the Southern Baptist Seminary in Louisville, Kentucky, over 400 miles away from my home in South Carolina.

While in seminary I met this pretty lady, Jane, who was spiritually on the same page as I. She was also devoted to let the Holy Spirit have His way with her, and we were married upon my graduation. We knew from the onset that we were really going to have to depend on the Lord, and we were inspired to do so. Our honeymoon consisted of a trip into Louisville with less than $25 to spare when we arrived.

> I'll say: "Yes Lord, yes" to Your will and to your way,
> I'll say: "Yes Lord, yes, I will trust You and obey.
> When Your Spirit speaks to me, with my whole heart I'll agree,
> And my answer will be: "Yes Lord, yes."
>
> Songwriter – Keesecker Lynn Edward

Since I was anxious to start my career as a pastor, someone referred me to a church about 50 miles up the Interstate that was interviewing for a full-time pastor. I was invited to preach there for three Sundays. There was then a vote by the parishioners, and I was greatly disappointed to learn that I was not selected. As it turned out, the Holy Spirit obviously intervened as we later learned of a situation that developed in that church that I would have been ill-prepared to deal with.

Another friend recommended me to a church even further away from South Carolina, to a loving congregation in Indiana. This small congregation was so kind to support and encourage me as a young preacher who was still learning to minister and to present sermons. As I pastored there for the next three years, Jane earned her PHT (Putting Hubby Through) degree by teaching school, while participating in ministering to the congregation. I worked on the grounds crew of the seminary to supplement my meager salary. After three years, the Holy Spirit worked on us with a desire to be closer to home in South Carolina, and he worked out the details for us.

A former school superintendent and personal mentor to me arranged for me to preach at my home church near our extended family. The church was seeking a pastor

through a pulpit committee, and another church also wanted to send their pulpit committee to check me out. The day before I was to preach, a member of yet another church, three hours away, ran into Jane's mother in local grocery store. In the conversation, he asked about me, her son-in-law, and whether I had finished seminary. She affirmed that I had and informed him that I was preaching the coming Sunday at her church. It turns out that he was a member of his church pulpit committee that was looking for a pastor. He then called my pastor for permission to send their search committee to hear me. When the time came for the Sunday service, my pastor added to my anxiety by announcing that I would be preaching before three pulpit committees. Whew!!

Following the service, one of the three committees slipped quietly out the door and departed. Another committee was kind enough to speak with me briefly before they also departed. The third committee, from the church three hours away, asked when we could come and talk with them. It just so "happened" that we had plans to visit Jane's parents the next day (translation: The Holy Spirit had gone before us). Later we scheduled a trial sermon from which I was accepted to become pastor of First Baptist Church of Venville, South Carolina. During this period of time, the Lord led us to adopt our infant son, Les.

Three rewarding years later, I received a call from a staff member from a church in an area of the state about 160 miles away. They were searching for a new pastor and wondered if we were interested in relocating. I replied that we were pleased where we were and not interested in a move. After praying about it for a few days, the Spirit encouraged us to leave the door open. We did so and then had eleven wonderful years at Latta Baptist Church. During that time, we adopted our daughter, Lynn.

The Spirit continued to move and opened a door in North Carolina. When this opportunity became known in our church, one of our parishioners, the school superintendent, asked me to come to the school. He had gathered some of our church leaders who then expressed the hope that we would not leave. One deacon said, "Those motorcycle gangs up there are dangerous." Although at the time we were uncertain of God's will for us, I responded that when the Lord called Abraham, he was obedient and "went to a land that he knew not of." An acquaintance, who was a circuit court judge, warned us that we were moving to the meanest city in North Carolina, Gastonia, about 200 miles away. The North Carolina committee said that they wanted us to come and love them just like they could tell that we loved the Letta Church. I felt, more than Jane, that the Spirit was leading us and so we accepted the position. For this, the third move, was during the days leading up to Christmas – a very difficult time! It turned out to be a great opportunity for us to continue to grow in our spiritual journey, and we were there for fourteen years.

It was a much larger church. The ministry was very rewarding and the salary was significantly higher. However, it was a challenge in so many ways, not just in our ministry, but our children had to relocate from a sheltered small-town environment to the city, and it was especially difficult for our son Les. But, as God would have it, Les eventually found his wife there and they and three of our grandsons are still in that vicinity. It was a very fulfilling assignment in every way, growing in my experience as a pastor and learning to minister in an urban community.

I have come to expect that, for those of us who truly want to serve the Lord, he continues to lead us on a journey that takes us away from our comfort zone and back on a path that is not clear where He is taking us or why.

Trust and obey for there's no other way
To be happy in Jesus, but to trust and obey.

The Spirit continued his work in us and a pulpit committee from a rural area in upstate South Carolina appeared unannounced. We were very attracted to this church and community from the onset. My passion was to minister to the smaller congregations as it can be a more personal relationship and not to have so many committees to work with and through. The downside of this relocation was that there would be a sizable cut in salary, going from a large church in an urban setting to a small one in a country setting. Jane would also be leaving a full-time job.

As we drove over to the Beaverdam Church, some 60 miles away, for the "trial weekend", we were impressed with the scenery, dotted with cows quietly grazing. Jane thought of Psalm 50:10 which states that the Lord says that He owns the cattle on a thousand hills, and she prayed, "Lord, if we come here and get in a financial bind, would you sell some of your cows for us?"

The next morning as I was preparing my sermon, Jane stood at the patio door of the pastorium beside the church. The back yard rose up towards a pasture fence. Beyond the fence, the pasture went downhill on the other side of the fence, so that she couldn't see into the meadow. As she stood there in meditation and prayer, she suddenly saw a cow at the fence. She and the cow gazed at one another and immediately there appeared another cow, then another and another . . . until about a dozen cows were lined up, looking into the yard. The Holy Spirit then gave her a thought as if He was saying, "Do you think this will be enough cows?" You know the end of this story – the Lord always provides plenty of cows.

And now for the most amazing part of this testimony. As we were serving as pastor in the Beaverdam Church, we were approaching the time for our retirement. One of the greatest dilemmas for most pastors at retirement is that they have been living in pastorium's and do not have a home to retire in or the funds to purchase one. My father, who was still living in the area where I was born, had purchased some property that included an old southern-style house with tall pillars on a front porch. As we approached retirement, he gave us the house that was about 50 miles away from my father. It had stood vacant, neglected and abused by transient renters for years. The yard was overgrown with weeds. Vines were growing inside the house, windows were broken out, the roof was leaking, and snakes dwelt in the attic. A room added on the back was falling in. The problem? $$$. Someone suggested that the way to save an old house was to start with $100,000. We, like most retiring pastors, did not have access to that amount of money. With the meager amount of retirement income, we could not afford a loan. We gladly accepted this gift from my father but had no idea how we could afford to make it livable. It turns out that this property had a history of an evil event and there were reports by others in the neighborhood of resident ghosts in the house. The exciting part of this story is what the Holy Spirit had plans for. He then displayed the fact that what others meant for evil, he would make good for his glory.

A sign out in front welcomed people to the McCravy Manor. John McCravy built the house in 1850 for his bride who, sadly, passed away during the birth of their second son in 1853. This was built on a cotton plantation and was a traditional mansion in those days. They, of course, owned slaves to work the fields, but instead of them living in separate shacks, they lived in the basement of this home, and prepared and ate the same food as the McCravys. John remarried and the second Mrs. McCravy purportedly said that she did not know what was for dinner until the food was brought up and served in the dining room. The relationship with the slaves was apparently very compatible. After the Civil War, the slaves were given their freedom and they could either leave or stay to work as hired hands. The grandfather in the slave family was too old to work and had nowhere else to go, so the McCravys let him stay and they would look after him, and the others moved away. Some of the locals objected to that arrangement and, when the McCravys were not there, they took the old man to a tree beside the house and hanged him. Their evil was made clear by the note that was left on the body: "Don't take him down. Let the buzzards have him."

The kind Mr. McCravy took him down and gave him a decent burial. That night, a delegation, wearing hoods and robes, rode up into the yard and called out McCravys name. Instead of going to the front door, he raised a window in the front room. The visitor's, thinking that he was at the front door, shot into the door. McCravy returned fire, and one of his "friends" walked with a limp the rest of his life. The bullet holes are still in the front door to this day.

Why were the locals already upset with the McCravys? There had been rumors circulating that a tunnel had been built from the basement to the nearby woods and the home and basement was part of the freedom trail for escaping slaves. The opening in the basement to the tunnel is still visible today. Some had speculated that he had helped several slaves to escape their abusive masters. It seems apparent that the Holy Spirit protected Mr. McCravy at the window when the night riders came up to "discipline" him. According to the New Testament, Jesus died on a cruel cross to give victory to his followers, giving them the Holy Spirit to protect them from evil and creating victories from such trials and tribulations of life. Sometimes the wind is against us, sometimes at our backs. But in the Spirit, we have peace, love and joy.

Fast forward to the 1950's when a large family occupied this old house. They told stories of ghosts moving things, making noises, walking down the hall with a candle in the night. One story was told by two young men, one of whom lived in the house. They drove their car up under an oak tree, looked up, and saw a man coming out of the front door wearing a long-tailed coat and a stove pipe hat. He walked across the front porch, down the steps, and disappeared when his feet touched the ground. Both men are still alive today and stand by their "story". Were these two men having the same hallucination at the same time? We cannot answer that. In Paul's writing in the Bible, he refers to "principalities and powers". We do know that Jesus has overcome the sinful world and his unseen Spirit indwells in believers who live in earthly houses. And we also know that Satan has unseen powers over people and events. We also are aware that in the Bible, John 16, that the Spirit always brings glory to Christ.

We began our reclamation of this home by having my dad bring his bulldozer and quickly remove the back room, which was too far gone to save. We then needed a new roof before beginning inside work, and we had just enough money for it even though we lost some of it with work promised but not done. We did as much as possible ourselves. When our front porch needed a new floor and replacement columns, the Spirit brought into our lives a carpenter who had grown up in the house, loved the place and restored it to its original design. Brotherhood men from our church in Beaverdam came repeatedly to help with the side porch and the bathroom floor. One of them, a retired electrician, hung all of the ceiling fans. Later, these men removed an interior chimney from the kitchen, took up two layers of the sagging floor, shimmed it, and replaced the wood. They then installed some old cabinets from another house, that had been in storage for twenty years. This same group returned three years after we retired, to build a back porch. When the Brotherhood worked on our home, we paid for the materials, they provided the labor, and we then made a contribution for their local projects. It was a win-win arrangement, we made some wonderful forever-friends, and the home was beautifully restored without a loan.

Step back to the time when we first began working on this old house. We used to hope that when the time came to get serious with this daunting project, that the Holy Spirit would provide a retired handyman who would enjoy working on our house - someone that we could afford. When we prayed, we never could have imagined that such a person would be Jane's own beloved stepdad, Warren Shipes. Her parents lived three hours away. Obviously, we could not have anticipated what the Spirit would do to answer this prayer. Well before the house was livable, Jane's mother died. Her dad was a good do-it-your-selfer and very handy. After losing his wife he was at loose ends, so Jane would drive to get him, and he would spend a couple of weeks working on our house. This went on repeatedly, even after we had moved into the house. He has now joined Mother in heaven, but we see and touch things everyday that remind us of all that he did.

It is amazing that we can look back and see that God was working, preparing us for a time such as this, in great detail and for years. His spirit was hovering, moving, waiting. In the 1860's, this old house witnessed an evil action resulting from an evil spirit, but saw Mr. McCravy delivered by the saving Holy Spirit. In the 1950's, the house was reported to possess ghosts. However, in the last thirteen years this old house and the Farmer family have been blessed by the powerful and loving Holy Spirit.

CHAPTER 17
A CATHOLIC GIRL AND THE HOLY SPIRIT

By Day Schwertman Lemming

The Catholic Church today is not the Catholic Church that I attended in 1935. I had spent twelve years in Catholic Church religion classes every day throughout my youth consisting of Bible stories and Catechism. We were told that the priest, at the alter, took the place of Jesus, and when he consecrated the elements, they became Jesus' body. In the first grade I received my first Holy Communion. I could hardly wait to think that I would be able to have a piece of Jesus for the first time.

Reading the Bible was not allowed, the explanation of which was that only the priest could interpret it. And again, it would also have been very difficult in that it was only printed in Latin.

We were also taught that we were not worthy to pray to Jesus, and therefore we needed to have an intercessor. We could and should pray to his mother, Mary, the Blessed Virgin, and that is what I did persistently. The month of May is the Month of the Blessed Mother and I always had an alter during that month in my bedroom, and I went to Mass and Communion at the church every day in that month. As often as I could, I said the Glory Be prayer between the 10 Hail Mary's between each bead on the rosary. At the end of each prayer, I made the sign of the cross, during which was the only mention of the Holy Spirit.

I grew up in Cincinnati, Ohio and after I was 10 years old my grandmother and grandfather would take me to Michigan to visit them, and her brother who was a Baptist minister. On Sunday's we would go to the Baptist Church, and therefore I would miss the Catholic Mass. I had been taught that by doing so I had just committed two mortal sins. I would then have to wait until the following Saturday to go to the Catholic Church for confession, to tell the priest of my sins. As a kid, I worried all week that, if I should die before I confessed my sins, that I was going to hell. My grandmother and mother had been converts to the Catholic Church and they didn't think that this was a big deal. It was so hard for me to understand that the Church was telling me one thing and the people that I loved telling another. There were times I would think, "what would Jesus think of me - that I love my uncle and cousins more than Him?" Maybe I should not go to the Baptist Church, but I did with *pure guilt!*

Then, in 1963 Vatican 2 happened and all of those sins that I had committed weren't sins anymore. I knew then that I had to study the Bible in order to determine what to believe and how to live a worthy life. In addition to this turmoil, I had more than I could handle going on in my life. I had married and had two small children, a son and a daughter that were very sickly, and my husband traveled all week, every week. The next year, I had to have my spine fused after experiencing years of pain. In the years after that, my husband had three serious operations in four years and eventually died in 1976.

At the time we were living in Cincinnati, and my husband had contracted leukemia. He was in and out of M.D. Anderson hospital, in and out of Critical Care several times. When he would come home, I would have to administer injections for the medications, and I was so worried that I might kill him doing something wrong. There were many trips in and out of the hospital that was many miles away. He finally was diagnosed with pneumonia and the antibiotics were not effective. The doctor said that the only way to know what to do for him was to operate and take a biopsy but patients would not usually recover. I told my husband that he had to make the decision as I just couldn't do it for him. He decided to go for it but the operation ended up in a horrible death.

For many years, I had experienced depression and had gone to a psychiatrist on and off starting in the 1950's. Unbeknownst to me, my mother hated me for my emotional instability and proceeded to likewise convince my family that I was not a good person, although she acted like she loved me. I thought my mother loved me as much as I did her. Nothing was apparent until the viewing for my husband. In the past, our family had always gathered at the person's home after the viewing, and I expected them all to come to my home. A couple across the street owned a bakery and had sent over donuts enough for the family. However, no one came – not my sister and her family that were in town from Michigan, and not even my parents showed up. After the funeral, my sister and family went directly back to Michigan. I later found out that my husband's younger brother was convinced and had told everyone that I had killed him.

At this time, I was 47 years old and had never expected to be alone without the man that I absolutely adored. I really had a hard time and went to counseling to find out what I had done wrong as even my friends left me. I had always been there for them when they needed help. I was advised that others have a difficult time dealing with death, and some women can feel threatened by a single female and their husband. After months of grieving and trying to get back to a new normal, for some reason I had a strong desire to have a picture of Jesus. My son, Joseph, had a friend, Gary Smith, who was an artist. I asked him to paint a picture of the Blessed Heart of Jesus, and he agreed to do so. He said that what he would really like to do was to paint the face of Jesus, as he was inspired to do. The resulting painting was an excellent rendition, and it has hung on my bedroom wall ever since 1981. I often refer to "my Jesus" in my conversation and in my prayers, it is this illustration that bring Him to mind.

In 1983 while living with my daughter in a very congested apartment in Cincinnati, friends invited me to move in with them along with my furniture. I soon realized that what they really wanted was not me but my furniture. I had no other place to go and after moving in I found that they were eating my food and there was little left over for me. I stated that I was paying my half of the bills, and if I don't have my own food, I couldn't continue to live there. I came home from the grocery store one day and there were three police officers waiting for me. They told me they wanted my gun, that I had hid behind my Jesus. They were standing behind me with their guns drawn and when I handed it to them, they determined that there were no bullets in it. They then demanded the bullets, and I retrieved them from the next room. They then put me in a police car and took me to a mental institute. I had to spend the next 72 hours there until going before a judge. Believe me, there were some genuine mental challenged people there! There was no TV and not much to do except put jigsaw puzzles together that did not have all of the pieces. There were no magazines and nothing else to stimulate our minds. If you were not crazy when you went in, this environment encouraged it. When the judge reviewed my case, he said that I could go but I needed to get the prescriptions that had been prescribed for me as I had been diagnosed as bipolar and had to take lithium.

I knew that they were wrong as I had been to a doctor for my depression years ago and bipolar was not the problem. I had to go back to court in 30 days and I had to see a psychiatrist of their choosing. I would not do that and instead I went to one that I knew would tell the truth about me. During those 30 days, however, I took their meds. When I went back to the judge, he realized that there was nothing wrong with me and set me free. Then I threw their drugs away. If I did not have My Jesus with me I, would have never been able to endure that time.

I had a very good job working at the University of Cincinnati in the financial aid department. I proceeded to call my boss and explained my circumstances. I had no idea how this was going to work out – would I be able to get my job back again. Amazing enough, thank you Jesus, he welcomed me back.

Much later that year I had a parking gate hit me on the back of my neck. I had previously been informed that their insurance would not pay for a knee operation that I needed, and now would not pay for this neck injury under workman's compensation even though this parking gate was on university property. An ombudsman gave me the name of an attorney to contact. I needed a small amount of money to hire him, which I did not have. My father stated that I would never win and my money would be wasted. I took another job outside of the university that was very hard work, but I endured for the three years while I could save enough money to continue the lawsuit. When you sue the university, you are actually suing the state of Ohio. I didn't ask for much money – all I wanted was enough for the cost of the operation. I was convinced that I would win as I was trusting My Jesus, and He knew that the university was wrong and I knew that my father was wrong. Sure enough I won the case, thank you Jesus!

In 1991 my daughter, Mary, had moved to Florida and was pregnant. The father of her child had died in April of that year. I had adopted Mary when she was young and I always felt that since I had chosen her, I had a larger obligation to help her in any way that I could. She obviously needed help so I moved from Cincinnati to Florida, a state that I had said that I would never live in. In August of that year, my grandson Bryce was born, and I adored him the second that I held him in my arms. I lived with them and took care of him all of the time. I taught him how to cook as soon as he was able to crack an egg. I was always teaching him something so, naturally, he loved me back.

Eventually my daughter didn't want me around anymore as she wanted to move in with a friend. I knew nothing about Florida, I have only one eye, I can not drive, and I had no place to go. I had made good friends with a couple in one of the apartments where we lived, Carol and Carl, but they had moved to Texas. They were aware of the way Mary had treated me, and kept telling me to come to Texas to live with them and they would take care of me for free, but I had to send them $400, which was all that I had. They wanted me to help homeschool their son. Carl came and got me and I took my furniture that I needed, including a cedar chest my husband had given me as our engagement present. They lived in Gradford, Texas, a very small town next to nothing.

The first month went well and then things started falling apart. Carol stopped my teaching her son that she had asked me to do. There was no church nearby for me to attend. They wanted me to paint the hallway, that I did, wash all the windows, wash the dishes including those when they had company. Eventually they informed me that they didn't want me to do anything else except the dishes, and I nearly went stir crazy! The weather turned very hot – up to 105 degrees outside – and there was no air conditioning. Every day I would take a walk with my Bible to a nearby cemetery where there was a bench, and I spent hours there. I also would walk down a road where I met a lady, and we became friends. I would take my phone and then Carl refused to let me make phone calls and took the phone away from me. I asked my new friend if I could use her phone and I would pay her for it, and she agreed. In that way, I could stay in touch with my daughter. By then, Mary was having trouble with her friend and wanted me back in Florida. On my birthday, Carl allowed me the use of my phone so that I could get in touch with my family, and then took it away again. I endured four months more of this treatment with the help of the Holy Spirit who led me to Mathew 6:34, 'Therefore do not worry about tomorrow, for tomorrow will worry about itself. Each day has enough trouble of its own." This verse is how I live my life to this day.

I then moved back to Florida, without my furniture, my cedar chest or My Jesus. I soon joined a nearby Methodist Church where I met Dean and his wife Katie. We participated in a Sunday school class and many church functions together and became good friends. Katie had invited her mother to move in with them as she was 95 years old and had no home. Katie was teaching in the church day school and Dean had an office in their home, trying to do business while also attending to Katie's mother. His business required travel throughout the country, and they really needed help in caring for their mother, so hired me as a caregiver.

I was always certain that somehow, in time, the Holy Spirit would make a way for me to again get my cedar chest and My Jesus back, but how? I was also convinced that the

Lord sends me angels when I really need them, and I realized that one of them was Dean. He had a business trip where he was driving to Texas and took his utility trailer with him in order to bring back my things. In that way, he went to Carl and Carol's home and proceeded to bring me my furniture, cedar chest, and My Jesus. What a blessing – thank you Lord! I still have them today in February 2023. If my husband would have lived we would have been married 73 years, and my cedar chest is a reminder.

In reflection, my faith has been very strong, and the Holy Spirit has led me through the good and bad times, over my troubled life, and is still very much with me. During the 9/11 tragedy my 91 year-old-mother was taken to the hospital in Cincinnati, and she really needed me. Although both Mary and I had jobs, we were barely earning enough to pay the bills, and I had nothing in savings to pay for my travel home to visit my mother. I had met another angel, who was willing to loan me $300 to get there. She has continued to be my permanent angel.

Soon after returning to Cincinnati, I purchased a computer as I am an experienced researcher in genealogy, and I am also an amateur author. The first time I needed service for the computer, I was charged $156 for the first hour. Later, when I had another problem, I knew that I could not afford such a charge. I found an ad in a local magazine for computer service, and to call "Ted". I did and when he answered and learned of my problem, he asked if I had a laser printer. I responded that I could not afford one. When he came to my door, he had a new printer. I replied that I had told him that I could not afford one, and he said, "Have you ever heard of "pay-it forward"? I had heard of the expression, and I was the beneficiary. As a genealogist and an author, there is a great amount of information that must be printed, and I could not live without it. I fully believe that he is another one of God's angels! And he never charges more than $20 a service visit, regardless of how long it takes.

Bryce has been a very devoted grandson and has done extremely well with his life. He is living in Florida, is a firefighter and trained to be a first responder in helping others in crisis. He recently flew up just to help me celebrate my birthday – 93 this year.

As I reflect back on my life, I have seen more that my share of troubles, but I have learned that in such troubles is where I see My Jesus' and the Holy Spirit always taking care of me, providing angels when I need them, and giving me a long and blessed life.

Day Schwertman Lemming

CHAPTER 18
MY LAZARUS MOMENT

Testimony by Jeff Kops

"OK Mr. Kops, we're going to start strapping you in now." The MRI technician had a mild Russian accent but her voice, even though direct and business like, still had a gentleness to it. "Once we get everything in place, it is very important that you stay absolutely still during the scan. This is going to take about 45 minutes". Wow, I thought, the nurse in the ICU said it would only take about 30 minutes. Immediately my nose started to itch, and I had this uncontrollable urge to scratch it. At this point, I think I was still in a mild state of disbelief that all this was happening. Barely 24 hours prior to this, I was living my life normally. For about the last month I was battling with what I thought was a persistent sinus headache that just wasn't going away, even after a trip into a walk-in clinic two weeks prior. I finally relented and saw an ENT, an ears, nose and throat specialist, and he sent me in for a CT scan to check out what was going on with my sinuses. I got the scan on a Thursday morning. The next morning I'm at my desk and the phone rings.

"Mr. Kops, this is the imaging center. The doctor has looked at your images, and you have a subdural hematoma (brain bleed). Have you fallen or hit your head lately?" "Um, no". This was getting serious. "We want you to get to the ER as soon as possible. St. Joseph's is the nearest hospital to you with a neuro ICU unit. If that's OK with you, we will contact them and alert them that you are coming in. Do you have someone who could drive you?"

2019 was just the latest in a string of rough years for me emotionally, financially, career wise and spiritually - especially spiritually. I gave my life to Christ when I was 9 years old during a summer vacation bible school in my hometown in Michigan. The seeds were planted, but as what often happens, they take time to truly take root. Although I stayed active in my church's youth programs through middle and high school, those years were spent mostly on sports, girls, and partying with friends. Once college started, church was no longer a part of my life at all, and it would be another 19 years before I came back. Fast forward to 1995. I had since graduated college, moved and lived in Dayton, Ohio for twelve years. I was married to Kathy, our son David was three, and a one-year old daughter, Sarah. Being born and bred mid-westerners and tired of freezing half the year, I sought and was blessed enough to find a position in Tampa for a year now. God also blessed me with a wife who insisted that our children be raised in a church home. So, at the recommendation of several of our new neighbors, we went to our local Methodist church and knew immediately we had found our church home. Although not a large church at the time, you could feel the Holy Spirit moving. The children's ministry was great, with a small day school that both the kids attended when they were pre-school age. Kathy plugged into the music ministry as she is a gifted singer and pianist. But for me, it was the men's ministry that appealed to me. I had never been around a group of guys that were so sold out to Christ. And in the midst of my new-found brothers, I recommitted my heart and soul to the Lord.

The next 20 years were spent as most young families - work, kids, school and for us being active members in our church. Kathy became a mainstay in the music ministry singing first in the choir and then out front on the praise & worship team. The kids participated in the youth programs and summer camps. I was involved in any number of ministries over those years as a volunteer or leader as well as serving on the church financial committee and church council.

The church grew quickly over those years (Praise God!), and of course lots of changes occurred. Most changes I agreed with, some not so much. Being a lay leader is a great honor but can also be a double-edged sword. I remember a fellow council member saying that although he loved serving, "Your perspective on your church can change once you go in the back room where the sausage is made." By 2016, our church was barely recognizable from the place we came to 20 years ago. Program changes in the music ministry disbanded Kathy's beloved choir and was going in a new direction. Both David and Sarah were young adults and leading their own lives. I was dealing with a drastic career change and financial challenges that left little time or energy for anything else. We made the decision that it was time to move on with the intention of looking for another church. But that intention never materialized. Despite everything I knew in my mind and in my heart about there being no such thing as a "Lone Ranger Christian" as our pastor used to call them, I set off into the desert with can of coke, ball cap and flip flops with the enemy whispering in my ear, "Don't worry, you'll be OK!" I made some half-hearted attempts to stay connected through periodically participating in a men's bible study and some various events, but for the first time in years, I was adrift.

To walk out of His will is to walk into nowhere."

C.S. Lewis

2019 started out with a lot of excitement and optimism concerning my career and finances. I had been a dental/medical sales rep for about ten years when my company was bought out in 2013. As what often happens, I was let go during the consolidation. Being in my mid-50's at the time, I had little chance of finding a new position in that industry. After a short stint trying to make it as an independent rep, a dear friend of the family met with me after church and proposed that I work with her at her property management realty company. I accepted and started out as a community association manager for a homeowner's association (HOA) and condo owner's association (COA). Discovering that this was not my calling, I got my Real Estate License and started on the property management and sales side of the business. I found this was much more inside my wheelhouse, but still not a passion. A new opportunity presented itself in 2018 when I met and got to know a trio of entrepreneurs that were putting together a patient/physician referral company involved in the burgeoning medical cannabis industry in Florida. My medical sales background was a good fit, so I was brought on to build our network of physicians. At Last! I was back in the medical arena, I had a salary, and I was in an industry with unlimited growth potential. We launched in January of 2019 with a fraction of the start-up capital we knew we needed, but our chief investment officer assured us that more capital would be flowing in and soon. Four months later, we had no capital, no investors, no more time, and no more salary. I worked with this group throughout most of 2019 as two more opportunities were presented and launched only to crash and burn. By October, the writing was on the wall that I had been a part of three failed start-ups in one year. That's got to be some kind of record. The excitement and promise of January had turned to the despondency and depression of October and November. I begrudgingly returned to real estate, signing on with a new company.

On top of all this, my father passed away in September. He had been suffering for years with a Parkinson's-like disease and had been in a long-term care facility for some time. We were never really close, but watching his slow deterioration was painful. I would not wish the last five years of his existence on this earth on my worst enemy. When he passed, I considered it a blessing, but at the same time, there were so many things that went unsaid that I regretted not telling him. And in my heart of hearts, I knew why. At this point in my life, my heart had atrophied into a piece of granite. I had all but shut off any grace and love provided by our Heavenly Father, and I was incapable of giving what I didn't have. The enemy did a masterful job in isolating me, making me feel alone, unwanted and unloved. If I prayed at all during this time, it was prayers of "why?" And Lord, just take me – I'm done. But the truth is, our Father is a good, good Father. He has a plan and I often joked that when the Lord needed to get my attention, he usually had to use a 2x4 across my head. Apparently, he took that analogy to heart.

To love at all is to be vulnerable. Love anything and your heart will be wrung and possibly broken. If you want to make sure of keeping it intact you must give it to no one, not even an animal. Wrap it carefully round with hobbies and little luxuries; avoid all entanglements. Lock it up safe in the casket or coffin of your selfishness. But in that casket, safe, dark, motionless, airless, it will change. It will not be broken; it will become unbreakable, impenetrable, irredeemable.

C.S. Lewis

"So, you don't remember hitting your head or falling?" I would be hearing this question again and again for the next few days. I was in the car with Susie, a neighbor and friend who was available to take me to the hospital. She was also a physician's assistant and neighborhood guardian angel. She was home with her husband who, coincidentally, just had knee replacement surgery a few days earlier. My wife, Kathy, was at work when I got the call to go to the ER, so Susie graciously volunteered to drive me in while Kathy met us at the hospital. As we talked, I realized that the last time I spent a night in a hospital was when I was around seven years old, to get my appendix out. It was the week before Christmas, and they released me Christmas eve. Today's date was December 20th. Once admitted, I was moved up to the neuro ICU unit which would be my home for the next three days. The nursing staff there was nothing short of wonderful, but I was a bit of an oddity in this world. Having a lucid, walking and talking patient amongst those suffering from strokes, massive head traumas and the like drew some quizzical looks from the staff when they met me. You could see the "What are you doing here?" question on their face the minute they walked into the room. My first morning there, I was in the middle of finishing getting dressed when the doctor came in to go over my CT images and discuss my case. Kathy had brought some pajama bottoms to me from home, and I was just finishing hitching them up when he walked in. He looked at me, smiled and said "Well, you're doing well today!" At first, I found it funny. Apparently, the bar is set pretty low here to be considered doing well. But on further reflection it revealed how blessed I was to be considered in a serious enough state to be here and still be able to function. The doctor went over my images and showed me what was going on. I didn't have one, but two hematomas, one on each side of my head. One was 1.92 centimeters deep, the other 1.10. He then informed me that 2.0 centimeters was the determining criteria for going in to take it surgically. My blood ran cold. My greatest fear after seeing my dad go through what he did was that this could be my fate. For the first time in my life, I was seriously dealing with my mortality. We discussed my case further, and in addition to my brain he wanted to get more detailed images of my neck area to check any possible issues there. So, he ordered an MRI and it was scheduled for later that evening.

"OK Mr. Kops, we're going to start strapping you in now." It felt much like I was being swaddled as the MRI technician took the blanket I was laying on and snuggly wrapped it around my body immobilizing my arms at my side. I did not feel claustrophobic, but it did give me pause when they placed a very close-fitting locator mask over my face. This was not going to be fun. The CT scans I had over the last few days were easy. Maybe 2 minutes in the tube which is relatively spacious and quiet. You are in and shortly you are out. An MRI is a different animal. 40 to 45 minutes without moving, in a tube small enough to where I thought my nose wasn't going to clear when they put me in. And oh yea, it makes noise - lots and lots of noise. But the thought that dominated my mind as they prepped me was how the process reminded me of the way a body was prepared for burial at the time of Christ. Perhaps it was the shock of finally understanding how close I was to losing almost everything, but in that piece of stone that once was my heart, something stirred. My mind went back to the story of Lazarus, and how once he died, his sisters had to wrap him in cloth and place him in a small tomb. Something in me could relate, I had felt spiritually dead for a long time. "OK Mr. Kops, we're about ready to start. We will be putting some headphones on you and you can listen to any soft music you would like. Just tell me who you want to listen to, and I can pull them up." Needless to say, I was fully unprepared for this. Who knew that they took requests? My mind was a total blank. With everything that had transpired over the last few days, I was lucky I remembered my own name, let along the name of a favorite artist. But before I could even process the question I heard a voice speak a name - a name I haven't uttered in years, whose music I haven't listened to in at least that long. "Chis Tomlin" I said. "Excuse me, who?" the tech replied. Again, I heard a voice: "C-H-R-I-S T-O-M-L-I-N". "OK, let me see what I can pull up on You Tube"

As the big machine was spinning up to start the scan, I knew I would go insane unless I had some way to mark time while laying motionless in the tube. So, I devised a way by counting the number of songs that I would be hearing during the scan. Some quick math based on a 3 to 4-minute song, and I'm looking at 12 to 15 songs. Great plan in theory, but once the scan got underway, I realized this was going to be much tougher to execute. These machines make noise. They buzz, they scream, at times it sounds like there is a guy outside the tube hitting it with a hammer. Any music that is on in your headphones is barely audible. But I was determined, I had to listen to the music. Then, as the machine progressed through its scan, occasionally there is silence. Its brief, but for just a moment you just hear the music, the lyrics, the message. God had a wonderful way of getting my attention as he needed to now, and by his grace, he finally got mine. As I laid there, I strained to hear through the noise and the chaos, the songs that were so familiar to me at one time. They were there, I knew them, but the outside noise would reduce them to where I could barely recognize them. But then the silence would come. Suddenly, unexpectedly, but oh so welcome. And each time the silence came, the message of the lyrics spoke to my heart and soul in ways I have never really experienced before.

Oh, I've heard a thousand stories of what they think you're like
But I've heard the tender whisper of love in the dead of the night
And you tell me you're pleased and that I'm never alone
You're a good, good father. It's who you are, it's who you are
And I am loved by you. It's who I am, It's who I am.

Chris Tomlin

Again, and again the noise would come, all but drowning out the message. But then the silence would come, the peace would come. The words of love and truth would flow over and through me, bringing my heart and soul back to life. I began to realize that the Lord was giving me the perfect analogy of what my life had been like over the past few years. I had decided to listen and get caught up in the noise, chaos and drama of this world. I listened to the lies of the enemy telling me I was alone in this, and that at this stage of my life there is little or no hope. But the truth was that in that time the Lord was there, gently calling, speaking to me. All I had to do was listen. When the scan finished, I literally felt like I had a Lazarus moment - I was dead going in, but Jesus called me out of the tomb of my own making, and I emerged alive and free.

I didn't get much sleep that night. You usually don't in a hospital, but this was different. The experience from earlier left me desperate for more. Thanks to the Lord and Google, I was able to access most of the music that I listened to back in the day through my cell phone. As I scrolled through the long list of songs, titles would literally jump off the screen. I would hit "play" and just listen, not only with my ears, but more importantly with my heart. Although I don't play an instrument and I couldn't carry a tune if I had a basket, the Lord uses music and lyrics to speak to me in ways I can't describe. And that night he had a lot to say. He reminded me of who I *really* am:

You are a child of Mine,
Born of my own design
And you bear the heart of life.
No matter where you go,
Oh, you will always know
You've been made free in Christ.
You are a child of mine.

I've heard the angels, and I've seen the devil
Fought with the lion, sent through the fire.
I've been in the valley, when it was dry,
Walked thru the desert, to the other side.

Through all these years, you have been there,
Dried all my tears, and answered my prayers,
I just wanna feel your presence again,
I'm down on my knees, in need of a friend,

And I find you waiting there for me,
and what you will continue to do for me through eternity.
And the chains around my heart fall away and break apart.
Suddenly you see, the truth has set you free.
When you're down, look around
And you'll see I am with you.
Take my hand and I can lead you on for you know:

I am the answer, and I am the way.
I am the promise, and I have called your name.

Interesting enough, these are the lyrics that came to me but as I research now, they are a combination of songs from Mark Schultz: You are a Child of Mine and I am the Way.

In every life there are certain moments that can be pointed to and because of events, circumstances or experiences, you can say "Here, this is where it all changed." For me, this is Dicken's Christmas Carol when he woke up from his night with the ghosts and realizes he is still alive, been given a second chance, and hasn't missed Christmas Day. I haven't felt that kind of joy in a long, long time, and through the grace of our Lord Jesus Christ, this joy is mine forever if I choose to stay close to him.

So here I am. I left St. Joseph's Hospital a month ago today and life has not been the same since. My concern was that this was all some kind of mountain-top experience that would wear off and down I would go again back to a "real life." Fortunately, it's been anything but that. One month later, I still am living a life that has been profoundly and irrevocably changed.

88

My mornings are different. Granted, the drugs that I am on have made it difficult to put in a full night's sleep. But, like Jesus, I'm up early these days and spend the first hour of my day in communion with the Father. During that time, I listen to powerful worship music, read scripture, journal and pray. This time has become sacred to me, and I literally can't wait to get out of bed in the morning.

My heart and my mind are different. Romans 12:2 says: "Don't copy the behavior and customs of this world, but let God transform you into a new person by changing the way you think." When I truly did that a month ago, there was a dramatic shift inside me. I am by nature and upbringing, an introvert. All my life I would rather have read a book or be by myself than actually interact with people. This experience has shifted me dramatically - God has truly opened my heart. I now *want* to meet people, hear their stories, understand them and help them if I can. I know I'm a *long way* from where the Father wants me to be, but I'm finally ready and more than willing to be led by His grace and the Holy Spirit.

My attitude towards my profession is different. As I said earlier, last fall I "begrudgingly" came back to real estate for my profession. I now consider this is yet another gift from the Father. It gives me the opportunity to help people in a powerful way while giving me the flexibility to go where the Holy Spirit leads me. Through prayer I feel that this is where the Father wants me to be at this point. So, I will be endeavoring through advanced training, coaching and experience to be the best realtor I can be. My dear friend, Dean Bates, told me that back when he had his own home repair and painting business, he proclaimed an agreement with the Lord. He said that he would do whatever he had to do to stay within His will as long as the Lord would do his marketing and scheduling. In that way, Dean wanted to go where the Lord wanted him to be, when He wanted him to be there and to do what the Holy Spirit expected him to do including ministering as He so directed and on His schedule. For Dean it was a wonderful experience for 19 years. For me, I went back to the Holy Spirit the next morning looking for the same arrangement in my profession!

Finally, you are reading what I consider the most miraculous evidence that the Lord touched me and is using me for his kingdom. The way this testimony has flowed out of me and on to this paper I am not capable of doing myself. I am not an author. I don't structure thoughts or flow the way this has come out. I am not this creative by nature. To be perfectly honest, (and yes, I know that I'm dealing with some brain issues here), I have written this early mornings after my time with the Father, and there have been times when words just flowed onto the screen. So, for the record if you get any inspiration, enjoyment or direction from this testimony, thank the Father for that. This is *for His Glory*! If he was gracious enough to reach down and touch an undeserving wreck like I was, he will meet you wherever you are!

CHAPTER 19
LORRAINE'S TESTIMONY

By Lorraine Standish

Yesterday, January 9, 2021, I talked on the phone to my sister Joan in Las Vegas, Nevada. For the very first time, we talked about our childhood. Long time coming, now that she is 85 and I am 83 years old. It's taken us this long to try to sort it out, confusing, troubling and infinitely complicated as it was. I have come to realize that a person carries his or her childhood with them for the rest of their life. So if you, the reader, have unfinished and unsolved business with your children, try to straighten it out if at all possible.

Our parents were Lucille Kenrick of Cambridge, Massachusetts and Harold Repetta of Medford, Mass., both beautiful people on the outside, but not on the inside. The Kenrick family is descended from the Pilgrims, but this is something we didn't know until recently. The Repetta's were probably descended from Italy. My sister, Joan was born in 1935 and I was born in 1937, both during the Great Depression. Our parents were not happy about it and I heard that an abortion was attempted on me but failed. This was very painful for a child to learn – never wanted, never really accepted. Mother often said to me, "I wish you'd never been born," but she didn't say this to my sister! However, we sisters were not jealous or resentful of each other. We were always close and still are. We turned out to be all that each other had after the divorce of our parents when she was five and I was three. We lived, briefly, with Mother and her female friend who had two little boys. I can remember that the boys bullied and fought with us, but we did not dare to complain. Back in the 1930's and '40's, children were not allowed to complain as you might get a slap in the mouth if you did. My mother would call me "Stupid", "Ugly" and completely unacceptable in every way. I would wonder, "What was wrong with me?" I never wondered, "What is wrong with her?"

My mother remarried when I was seven and my sister was nine, and we then went to live with them in New Hampshire. Our father still lived in Massachusetts, and we went to visit him every other weekend. We traveled either by bus or by train. Dad must have paid our fare, and my sister and I always traveled alone. In those days two pretty little white girls could travel along and be safe. When visiting dad, we stayed with his mother and father that was also where he was living until he got an apartment of his own.

His girlfriend would try to win us over, when we were there, hoping that dad would then marry her. He didn't remarry, however, until 20 years later – long after we were both married and living out of state.

When I was 10, my mother then had my stepsister that I loved very much! As a baby I took her everywhere with me, partly to have an excuse to get out of the house and away from my mother.

I was terrified of my mother. Once in the middle of the night she pulled me out of bed and beat me up without explanation. I figured out later that she had apparently read a letter that I had written to a friend but had not yet sent it, informing her what was going on.

After that, we sisters were separated for a while as we lived with different relatives in different places in Massachusetts. Nobody seemed to want us. We didn't realize it at the time, but we were two more mouths to feed during the Depression. We only knew that nobody wanted us, and nobody seemed to love us. At least we had each other but we never talked about our situation,

When I was 17 with one more year of high school to go, I met a Navy man at a dance who was 22 years old. We dated for a few months and then decided to get married. I invited him to dinner with my mother, stepfather and little stepsister. At the table my mother, for no apparent reason, became upset with me and raised her hand to strike me in the face while saying, "When you were born, they threw away the baby and saved the afterbirth." Oh, that was probably the worse thing she ever said – and said it in front of my fiancé and family. My fiancé, Myles, grabbed her hand, looked her in the eye and said, "Leave her alone!" and she did! I have often wondered if I had stood up to her sooner, would she have left me alone? I am convinced, however, that she would have carried through with her oft-repeated threat that she would have killed me if I ever told anyone about her abuse. This is why, even though she is no longer living, that I am shaking as I am writing this at age 83.

Myles and I soon left the house after dinner, and he held me in his arms to help comfort me. He asked if I would like him to pay my way to Arkansas so that I could live with his mother and grandmother. I originally declined as my desire was to go to Dover, New Hampshire to graduate with my class but I never got there as my mother moved to Florida for a job, and I would have had no one to stay with. About the same time Myles completed his commitment with the Navy, so we got married by a Justice of the Peace with only one of my friends present. We then moved to Arkansas to live with his mother and grandmother. I had never met them, of course, but his mother was very relieved to see her son married and settled. She fully accepted me, a 17-year-old child, as a daughter that she never had. She never said much of anything about Myles' father.

Myles enrolled at the University of Arkansas that was nearby, and I was able to get work to support him with his educational expenses, including his master's degree in electrical engineering. At that time the space program was in its infancy and Myles joined them in Huntsville, Alabama where we lived. During his career he became a noted rocket scientist and life was very good. We had two beautiful girls that graduated from college but remained single.

Myles had grown up without a father figure in his life and his mother had to work while his grandmother took care of him. We later found out, after his mother died, that he was conceived out of wedlock while his father was married to another woman with two teenaged children of his own. Myles' mother then moved from New Hampshire to Arkansas to live with her mother and grandmother.

Now, this is the first time that I have mentioned my spiritual life. I always knew that there was a God, but I didn't go to church or read the bible. Myles and I didn't go to church even though he had grown up in the Presbyterian church with his grandmother. But when he retired, we found a nice retirement home in southern Alabama and we met up with an old friend of Myles. The friend talked us into helping build a Methodist church in the area and we started attending. Much to our surprise, we loved it! It became the family that we never had – men, women and children who really cared about us. We learned that this was God's plan for us all along as with Him there are no coincidences. And now I thank God for being a loving God. He inspired me to become an author and poet – even teaching creative writing at the University of West Florida that was nearby even though I didn't have a degree. I have had many, many short stories and poems published, but I would not have been qualified to write them without Him bringing me through the emotional trauma and corresponding healing in my life.

For you see, this is not a happily-ever-after story. Neither Myles nor I were brought up in a loving and caring environment with parents to emulate.

As a mother, I was easily angered and often yelled at our daughters. I never, however, physically or emotionally abused them. Myles was an excellent provider but did not have a warm and friendly personality with a confident relationship with his daughters. In hindsight, it is apparent that the emotional baggage from childhood had a direct effect on both of us as parents – never able to show love and affection to each other and in the family. Neither one of our daughters ever married. One of them died of alcoholism in 2005 and the other one died from breast cancer in 2006. In 2007 I also had breast cancer that fortunately was successfully treated. And then in 2011, Myles died and at that point my life was shattered. About two years later, I married a neighbor that I had known for many years but within two years he too died. After all of these tragedies, I became severely depressed. I remained despondent until a distant relative of mine suggested to Dean to contact me and invite me to participate in this book – both as a contributor as well as proofreader. Although we have never met, through this endeavor the Lord brought me back to an inspired life with joy and purpose. Thank you Lord – amazing grace!

GOD'S GRACE

By Lorraine Standish

He said, "Love one another"
     "How can we do that?" we asked.

He said, "Pray for each other."
     We said, "That's too big a task."

He said, "Be sure that your vine is entwined with Mine."
     We said, "We don't need you, Lord – we're just fine."

We paid no attention to what He would say,
     Lived our own life and went our own way.

"Be still and know that I am God." He said.
     But we tried to get to know ourselves instead.

We found pain and misery wherever we went,
     Searched the world over but were never content.

And when we were shattered, battered and broken,
     Only then we remembered the words He had spoken,

Until we reached out our hand to touch His sweet face,
     And then, through His forgiving grace
     He put all the pieces back into place.

He took all the bad times and turned them to good,
     And then, only then Lord – WE FINALLY UNDERSTOOD!

By Lorraine Standish

TO MY CHILDREN

While still in the womb you kicked at my heart,
       And knitted yourself into my bones.

You became a part of my blood and sinew,
       And I could not begin to tell where I ended and you began.

And now so many, many things, places, times, experiences and years,
       Have passed between us – together and separately,

But I am still a part of you, and you are part of me.

By Lorraine Standish

CHAPTER 20

CORDEL'S TESTIMONY

Personal Experiences with The Holy Spirit: How He Has Guided and Protected Me

By Cordel Batchelor

1. Introduction: How My Relationship Started with the Godhead: God the Father, God the Son and God the Holy Spirit

MY MOTHERS DECISION TO LEAVE FOR ENGLAND

In the late 1940's after World War II, Britain was short of workers. They needed to recruit thousands of workers from the British West Indies. Life in Jamaica was extremely hard at that time. My mother decided that this was the opportunity of a lifetime to join the thousands of workers who were going to London to find work. She was intentional. Her goal was to carve out a better life for her two children. She was young, approximately 30 years old. Looking back on her decision, I have always admired her bravery and determination. In Jamaica she owned her own dress-making shop and my father owned a bar next to her shop. Business was not good, and the marriage was even worse. She decided to leave my sister and me with her mother and her two sisters, and take off for London, England.

My mother loved the Lord but only attended church twice a year, Easter and Christmas. My grandmother Lilian, on the other hand, never missed a Sunday at church. We all had to attend church from the time we were babies. She loved the Lord, she had a close relationship with Him, and she had strong faith in God. Her husband (my grandfather) passed away when she was approximately 45 years old and left her with 8 children (including my mother) to raise on her own. I was very close to my grandmother and as I got older, I would ask her personal questions about her life that, for some reason, none of her children ever seemed to ask. She told me that as my grandfather's illness got worse, she was worried about her future even though he left her with a 30-acre farm and 5 farm hands. As she sat by his bed when he was dying, she said, "Charlie, what am I going to do when you are gone?" He held her hand and told her not to worry, and quoted Isaiah 41:10 (one of my favorite scripture verses) " . . fear not, for I am with you, be not dismayed, for I am your God, I will strengthen you, I will help you, I will uphold you with my righteous right hand." After he quoted that verse to her, he told her to put her hand in God's hand and God would look after her. Later that evening he passed away and went on to heaven to be with God.

The Moravian Church: Its Legacy in the Caribbean:

My grandmother's family attended Fairfield Moravian Church in Jamaica. That church is over 200 years old, and it is still standing in Fairfield, Manchester Allow me to digress, and tell you about my Moravian heritage. Most people have no idea about Moravians, and some think they are a cult. I am very proud of my Moravian heritage, and you will see why. The Moravians came from Germany to Jamaica, and are one of the oldest Protestant denominations in the world dating back to the 15th century. They were closely aligned with the Methodists and laser focused on missionary work. As such, they were the first Protestant missionary movement to take the gospel to the Caribbean, North and South America. Because Fairfield happened to be one of the places where the Moravians settled in the Caribbean our community had the privilege of excellent education from elementary school through college. Everywhere that they settled around the world they built elementary schools, high schools and colleges. The impact that this had on every community around the world was phenomenal. I had six grand aunts who were born in the late 1890's and early 1900's. Four of them graduated from Teacher's Training College administered by the Moravians. My youngest great aunt Ada died last year at the ripe old age of 105 years. She taught for 50 years in the classroom. She taught day and night. When she realized that there were many adults who could not read or write, she started adult literacy classes at night. In her lifetime, she taught hundreds of adults to read and write in her village. That was the legacy of the Moravian Church. They were not as well-known as other denominations because their emphasis was on developing and making a significant difference in the communities where they were planted all over the world through emphasis on education and other missionary work.

MY INTRODUCTION TO LEARNING ABOUT GOD

I was two years old when I started attending church every Sunday with my grandmother. Attending church and Sunday school classes was my first introduction to hearing about the "Triune Godhead," God the Father, God the Son (Jesus) and God the Holy Spirit. At that age I knew very little about the Triune God, but I enjoyed the wonderful bible stories and heard and sang how much "Jesus loved the little children of the world whether yellow, black or white all are precious in His sight. I never forgot that. It was comforting as a child to know that Jesus loved me.

I left my grandmother when I was eight years old and I went to live with my aunt in Kingston, Jamaica. When I was ten years old, I attended an Easter Service at the North Street Moravian Church. Children did not enjoy attending Easter Services back then. The Service was three hours long and, if you forgot to bring a snack, the hunger became unbearable. And what was even more unbearable, and embarrassing was the loud growling sound that my stomach made. The entire row of church folks could hear. But this Easter Service was different. I happened to be listening to every word that the Pastor was preaching and what he preached that Sunday changed my life forever. During that service, the pastor told me that Jesus died on the cross to save me from all my sins. I remembered being moved by the fact that Jesus loved me so much that He died such a terrible death on a cross for me. My life was never the same after that sermon. I decided that if Jesus could do that for me, I could dedicate my life to Him. So, I did. I

attended a series of classes where you study the bible. After those sessions come to an End there is a special ceremony in church where you declare Jesus as your Lord and Savior and vow to abide with Him for the rest of your life.

MY YEARS IN LONDON, ENGLAND

In 1969 I left Jamaica for London, England to live with my mother. I was 16 years old, and I had a very close relationship with the Lord. I knew about the Holy Spirit based on what I read in the bible, heard in Sunday school classes and in sermons. However, I did not have a relationship with the Holy Spirit as I had with God the Father and Jesus. Little did I know at the time that although I did not know the Holy Spirit, He knew me and He was guiding, protecting and giving me wisdom in those crucial years when I needed it.

My first winter in England was extremely cold and lonely. I had left all my friends behind coming to a new world with all its challenges. Although my mother was one of the most loving mothers that any child could have, my mother and my sister worked long hours and I was in this huge house all by myself much of the time. During that first winter I decided that I would never live in England longer than I needed to. It was way too wet, cold and dreary for me. I told my mother that as soon as I completed my education, I would be leaving them for Jamaica.

During those teenage years, I missed not having a father to talk to especially when life got lonely. I had no choice but to draw even closer to God. I asked Him questions about my past, present and future. One of the questions that I asked was why I did not have the privilege of knowing my father. (My grandmother went against my mother's advice and never allowed my sister and me to see my father after my mother left for England). God's answer to me was clear. God reminded me that He was my "heavenly Father and He would take care of me. I believed Him. I never forgot those words and the moment that I spent with Him that day. He immediately became not just my heavenly Father but my "Abba Father." I drew even closer to Him because He was the only Father that I had. There were many days when I visualized myself climbing into His lap and having a conversation with my Abba Father. As I mentioned above, I knew that God was guiding me, protecting me, and giving me wisdom. At the time, I did not realize that it was the Holy Spirit, but I made the connection years later.

Fast forward, I stayed in England nine years and accomplished all my goals. I completed my education. I received a Bachelor of Science Degree in Social Science and a master's degree in Industrial Relations. I returned to Jamaica that year and worked for an American Mining Company as an Industrial Relations Specialist. I knew without a doubt that I could not have achieved all of this without the help of the Holy Spirit.

COMING FULL CIRCLE, BACK TO JAMAICA

In 1978 I returned to Jamaica. It took a lot of courage to leave my mother and sister in England and return where I had no family except my grand aunt Ada and her two children. All my other relatives were living in the United States. In Jamaica, I picked up where I left off in 1969 and started going to bible study on Wednesday nights and church on Sundays. I say this because one of my many regrets while I lived in England was that I never attended church. I never extended my search for a church beyond my neighborhood. Looking for a church should have been a top priority, but it was not, and I eventually gave up searching.

Back in Jamaica at bible study, I started learning more about the Holy Spirit. I got married in 1981 and had my first son in 1983. Things were going very well, and I enjoyed living in Jamaica. In 1985 after spending approximately 7 years in Jamaica, the mining company where my husband and I were employed closed. We (my husband, son and I) decided to leave Jamaica and join my husband's father in Tampa. I enjoyed my stay in Jamaica tremendously, but it was time to move on.

USA, MY NEW HOME

Within four years of arriving in Tampa, I had three more children including twin boys. I was a stay-at-home mom with four children. Once again, I needed to draw close to my Abba Father, Jesus and the Holy Spirit. One day as I was working in the house, I invited God to start speaking to me like He did to Moses. He answered my prayers and started speaking to me. This was how that conversation went. "Lord, how come you do not speak to me like you did to Moses? I know that in Your eyes I am the same as Moses, no less". God spoke to my spirit; This is what I heard Him say. "I speak to you, but you cannot hear me because there is too much noise in the house." I agreed. The television was always on and loud. After I heard His voice, I started turning the TV off regularly. The house was quiet, and I grew accustomed and enjoyed hearing His voice more and more. I remember telling members in my adult Sunday school class in Tampa that God speaks to me, and He speaks to all of us if we will listen. I was the laughingstock of my class that morning and only the Sunday school teacher came to my rescue. Ann was about 78 years old and spent most of her adult life communing with God. She knew exactly what I was talking about. I was about 40 years old at that time and we became good friends until she passed away.

GETTING TO KNOW THE HOLY SPIRIT

As I studied the word of God, I started to know more about the Holy Spirit. I knew there was something special about Him. He gave me wisdom to make decisions. He answered some of my questions even before I completed the questions. He gave me strength, power and perseverance to never give up in so many situations that I faced. The Holy Spirit also revealed to me how He protects me from the enemy whose plan is to destroy me. I know beyond the shadow of a doubt that the enemy is real and that he tried to take my life several times (see my testimonies below), but I also knew that "greater is He who is in me than he who is in the world." 1 John 4. Every time the enemy tried to take me out, the Holy Spirit was there to protect me.

As I got to know more about the Holy Spirit I started looking back at the chapters of my life, growing up in Jamaica, then in England, returning to Jamaica, getting married having children, moving to Tampa, changing careers and battling breast cancer (see below). There was something that remained constant through the good times and the trials and I knew the presence of the Holy Spirit was constantly watching over me.

WHO IS THE HOLY SPIRIT?

Many experiences led me to start getting closer to the Trinity, especially my unbelievable miracle with cancer that I will discuss below. I have asked the Holy Spirit to tell me everything about Himself - all the things He did for me. His response was remarkably simple: He told me to read,, ponder and understand what Jesus said as He was about to leave us on earth. I went boldly and read the passage, John 14 :16-17. Jesus said that He would ask the Father to give us a Helper to be with us forever. He would be the Spirit of Truth. Jesus went on to say that the world could not receive Him because the world does not see Him or know Him, but we will know Him because He will be with us and in us. That passage that I read for years in church and out of church just took on a new meaning and importance. The Holy Spirit is as important to me as Jesus. He is Jesus' representative on earth. Imagine how awesome that is! When we think of how fortunate the disciples and all the people in the bible were to have Jesus, the woman at the well, Lazarus, Mary and Martha, the woman with the issue of blood, to name a few. How we have Jesus's' representative, the Holy Spirit with all the attributes and more of Jesus. The reason I say "more" is because Jesus could only be in one place at a time where the Holy Spirit can be everywhere at the same time. Amazing! Awesome! It is liking having millions of dollars in the bank and going around thinking that you are poor because you have not tapped into the resources that you have. My apologies for that feeble analogy. We have the Holy Spirit, yet we know so little about Him and what He does for us.

After reading these verses again, the Holy Spirit helped me to see and understand that He does everything for us on earth that Jesus did while He (Jesus) was here with us. Our relationship with the Holy Spirit should be the same as it was with Jesus. He interceds for us, guides us, protects us from danger, teaches us, gives us wisdom, leads us into all truth, prays for us, teaches us, empowers us, convicts us. He speaks to us by promptings in our spirit. The more we are aware of these promptings and obey His voice, the clearer and more frequently we hear Him.

2. The Holy Spirit Heals and works His Miracles In Our Lives

In 1997 I was diagnosed with breast cancer. Between 1997 and 2005 the cancer returned four times in my body. It returned under my left arm, in my left collar bone, under my right arm and at the back of my neck behind my left ear. Each time it returned the doctors used the phrase "metastatic cancer, stage 4" Imagine hearing this four different times over an eight-year period. I knew that was not good! Over this period, I was given five extraordinarily strong cocktails of chemotherapy. In 2005 my doctor told me that I would have to take chemotherapy for 10 years non-stop as maintenance. I wondered how I would tolerate it for 10 years. This cocktail was very strong. Many individuals, including a close girlfriend of mine, could not tolerate its strength. Their doctors had to take them off this chemo, and two months after that my girlfriend passed away. I was very sad, but it was incidents like this that opened my eyes to the miracle that God was performing in my body.

As I mentioned above, the cancer returned four times. I had to take chemotherapy three Saturdays a month for 10 years. Although the actual therapy lasted three hours, I would spend approximately five hours at the hospital each Saturday. After many years of this routine, I remembered driving into the hospital and asking the Lord if I was ever coming out of this place alive. Although my faith was strong, there were days when my faith waivered but only for a few seconds. I knew the Lord would take care of me and I kept praying and holding on to His promises. Those days when my faith waivered for seconds, the enemy would try to speak to my spirit and tell me that I was going to die. As soon as I heard satin's voice, I would speak back to him like Jesus did and I would do so immediately! I would answer satan with one of God's promises in the bible. (Note that I refuse to capitalize satan's name. He will always be a lower-case "s". The grammar check on my computer is going nuts because I refuse to capitalize his name.) One of my favorite verses as I answered satan was Psalm 118:17. "I will not die, instead I will live to tell what the Lord has done." I tried to stay strong in my faith and I always prayed to have joy. During those years I probably cried a total of less that one hour. I know it is hard to believe but it is true. My husband, my four children, my workmates and my close friends can attest to that truth. Each time the doctor gave me a bad report, I would cry in my car for about five minutes or less, then I would hear God's voice asking me this question, "do you believe My word that I am God of the impossible?" and my answer would always be a resounding "YES". As I settled that score, I would drive home with joy. God's promises kept me going through all the bad news and through the years.

I never knew the answer to that question above. "Lord am I ever coming out of this hospital alive?" but the Holy Spirit did. All I needed to do was to trust Him and be patient. I kept praying throughout those years for miracle healing. Not only did God, Jesus and the Holy Spirit heal me, but I experienced many astounding miracles over that period. Here are some of the miracles that I experienced over that 18-year period. (1) I never vomited, not once. (2) I was never sick or in pain one day. Not even after one of my surgeries that lasted nine hours. It was a breast reconstruction (Tram Flap) surgery where they had to take a piece of my stomach to reconstruct my left breast. Wow! I was able to go to work every day and I never missed a day of work except when I had the three surgeries or had doctors' appointments. Everyone around me witnesses these incredible miracles including my boss, my co-workers, my church family, my family and my friends.

In 2015, the doctor told me that because I had been cancer free for ten years, she was taking me off chemotherapy. No one could imagine the joy and the gratitude I felt that day! It has now been eight years since I received that good news for which I have been praising and thanking God the Father, Jesus and the Holy Spirit daily.

3. The Holy Spirit Knows All Things and Reveals Them To Us

"Call upon me and I will answer you and will show you great and mighty things that you do not know."

Jeremiah 33:3

I knew this verse in Jeremiah from a young age, but I had to exercise my faith and believe every word of this promise when I decided to change career is my late 30s. I was an Industrial Relations (IR) Specialist in the Human Resources Department. I enjoyed that career very much, but I wanted to become a Lawyer. I was accepted by two universities in Florida, and I decided to accept the law school that was closest to my home in Tampa. I entered law school with four children including twin boys. I knew law school was not going to be easy, but I was determined. I started law school in 1991 and found that I was in over my head. I realized very early that I desperately needed the Holy Spirit to help me and give me wisdom, guidance and understanding.

My journey and experience with the Holy Spirit in law school was amazing and one that I will never forget! Now, this story may sound crazy, but it is true. My only explanation for what happened in this experience with the Holy Spirit is that God loves to do the unusual things to remind us that He is can!

Studying would have been so much easier if I had organizational skills, but I did not. In 1992, in my second semester I had a Property law exam that was only a few days away and I was definitely not prepared for it. I was downtown Tampa in the law library, feeling sad and disappointed with my lack of preparation for this important exam. In my desperation I did the usual thing that I have done all my life, I called upon Father God, Jesus and the Holy Spirit to come to my rescue. I told the Holy Spirit that I knew that He was omniscient, all knowing. (The bible taught me that and I believed it). I told Him that I knew that He already knew the questions that the professor prepared for the exam, and I would like Him to tell me what those questions were. It was my first and hopefully my last time being so desperate, and I apologized for being so presumptuous.

I told the Spirit that I needed His help in order to continue towards my new career, otherwise it would end. I knew that the exam consisted of two essay questions and forty multiple choice questions. I asked Him to reveal to me what the two essay questions were. I remember being so desperate that I had no choice but to believe that God would answer my prayer and so my desperation helped my faith if that makes sense. If God did not answer my prayers my law school career could be over

As soon as I was finished praying, my spirit immediately received a prompting that the two questions would relate to the subject of "the Rule of Perpetuities." This area of property law was antiquated and was an unlikely topic to be on the exam. I say "antiquated "and "unlikely" because I was told by senior students and professors that it was highly unlikely that this topic would ever be on a law school exam.

So, let me break this down. The Holy Spirit answered me and told me that the two questions related to the Rule of Perpetuity. In that moment I was very upset and disappointed. I had reason to believe that I was not really hearing from the Holy Spirit because senior students and professors said that it was very unlikely that topic would ever be on a property law exam. Knowing this and feeling frustrated, I grabbed my book bag and started down the stairs to go home. Immediately I heard a voice almost shouting at me telling me to go back upstairs and be obedient to what I heard. I decided to obey the voice. I went back upstairs and read two books on the Rule of Perpetuities and took copious notes. When I left the law library that evening, I was still despondent, but I was confident that I knew everything I needed to know about the Rule.

On the day of the exam, I reluctantly opened my exam "blue book." The first question I read I had no idea how to answer. I tried not to go into panic mode because that would only restrict the blood flow to my brain and make things worse. I was afraid to turn to the back of the book to look at the second question. Next, I decided to answer the multiple-choice questions. After completing these multiple-choice questions, with fear and trepidation I gingerly turned the page to look at the second question. The second question said, "if you had to change one of these rules, how would you change it and why. Rule No.1 the rule of Perpetuity. and Rule No. 2 Shelly's Rule. I was shocked because I was told that this topic would never be on the exam. But I was ecstatic because I was more than prepared for this question and I "tore it up." I wrote so much that I needed another "blue book." The grades came out the next day and my grade was a C+. I was so happy to get a C+ you would think I got an A grade.

I called my professor for an analysis of my exam, as I always did. The analysis that my professor gave me was astounding! He told me that my second question was perfect and jokingly said that it was so good that one day he would invite me to teach his class on "The Rule of Perpetuities." He told me that he was very puzzled that I got a zero on the first question because both questions were related to the "Rule". In speaking to him, I realized that on the day that he taught the class that was related to the "Rule", I realized that on that day I was late for class, and I did not follow up on getting the handouts or the notes relating to that class. So, that is why I did not know anything about that question.

This experience with the Holy Spirit was amazing! To think that the Holy Spirit was spot on! I thanked the Spirit, that I could not believe that He heard my prayer and answered it precisely. This experience changed my life and grew my faith tremendously! I no longer wrestle with questions such as, "does God hear me when I pray?" I know for sure that God hears us and that the Holy Spirit speaks to us and reveals things to us with promptings in our spirit This experience was so "crazy" that I questioned whether I should include it in this testimony. In the end, I decided to include it because as unbelievable as it may seem, it really did happen. It was another jaw dropping moment with the Holy Spirit and It was a pivotal moment in my knowledge and relationship with the Spirit. Over the years as I pondered on how the Spirit came to my rescue and answered my prayers, I concluded that God really does have a sense of humor as I think He takes delight in answering some of these requests that we think are impossible in order to show us who He is and to increase our faith. I was learning more about Him, the powers that He has and the fact that just as He states in His word, He is Omniscient, (all knowing) and nothing is impossible with Him. He is the God of the impossible!

I graduated from law school and practiced for 20 years as a criminal law attorney. During those years, the Holy Spirit was always with me teaching me, guiding me and giving me wisdom. As a trial attorney, I always invited Him to be with me during all my trials in the courtroom and I always felt His presence and assurance.

4.   The Holy Spirit Gives Us Rhema Words

What is a "Rhema word?" According to Wikipedia, rhema is defined as "God's Word Spoken to You". A Google search defines "Rhema literally means an "utterance" or "thing said" in Greek It is a word that signifies the action of utterance. Google further states that rhema is a specific word which the Holy Spirit quickens in our hearts and minds at a specific time and for a specific purpose. We receive a rhema word from the Spirit when He specifically wants to remind us of a particular Bible verse or promise and drops the "word" into our heart.

Rhema words are usually profoundly wise, so wise that you want to run for pen and paper to write it down before you forget it. It is usually so enlightening that you know that it is a rhema word from God. Rhema words never contradict God's word, and it is usually given to make you a better person. It is always said with clarity, wisdom and profound truth. You may get it from the Holy Spirit at any time when you are praying, when you are meditating, reading the word of God, when you are praying, when you are memorizing scripture, when driving a car or even in the shower. Years ago, the Spirit would speak to me profoundly as soon as I stepped into the shower, I was so amazed that I started a journal called "Wisdom from the Shower". Over the years I kept a notebook and pen close to me so that I would never miss those moments.

This is my example of a rhema word. This word was given to me by the Holy Spirit at a time in my life when it felt like the walls were closing in on me and I really needed spiritual advice. Not only did I receive a word from Him, but it changed my life and the way I related to everyone. It was a rhema word that I will never forget, and I hope it helps you too.

My Ephesians 6:12 Rhema Word

"For our struggle is not against flesh and blood,
but against the rulers, against the authorities,
against the powers of this dark world and,
against the spiritual force of evil
in the heavenly places."

There was a season in my life when I was being attacked (not physically) by two people. I was praying for years and asking the Lord to help me with their negative comments about me. I was struggling with unforgiveness against these individuals. I am serious about forgiveness because it is so crucial to being in a righteous, holy relationship with God. In Mark chapter 11, Jesus says "whatever you ask in prayer, believe that you have received it, and it will be yours. And whenever you stand praying forgive, if you have anything against anyone, so that your Father also who is in heaven may forgive you your trespasses. (Mark 11:24-25) I have taken these verses seriously. So, over the years I kept praying to forgive those two individuals. One day the Holly Spirit gave me a rhema word regarding Ephesians 6:12. These are the words He said to my spirit. Cordel, "Do not look at flesh and blood as your enemy. Do not see these individuals as your enemy. Look past them and realize that they are vessels being used by these spiritual forces of wickedness in heavenly places who are trying to attack you." The Holy Spirit continued speaking to my spirit: You are in a spiritual battle, not a physical battle and satan is working through them to attack you. The important thing for you to understand is that the enemy will use anyone on any given day to attack you and that is why you should not be upset with individuals, with flesh and blood, . The enemy will use a family member, a co-worker, a friend. In fact, the enemy will sue even you on some days if you are not prayed up and walking in and with the Spirit. This is exactully what the Holy Spirit spoke to my spirit.

Wow! I began focusing on being empowered by the Holy Spirit to stand up against these attacks. You know you are doing something good in God's kingdom when these evil forces are on the attack, so you must stay connected in the word and in the Spirit. I was able to stop focusing on and being upset with those individuals There were days when it was not easy but the Holy Spirit would remind me of Ephesians. That explains how that rhema word helped me in my relationship with those individuals, and with people in general. I stopped focusing on the way individuals treated me and started focusing on not being upset. There were days when it was not easy, but the Spirit would remind me of Ephesians 6:12, and this made it easier to accomplish.

Another amazing change that happened was that my prayers for these two individuals were more sincere because I realized they were being used as pawns by these evil spiritual forces of wickedness. I made the decision at that time that I would not waste any more time and energy being upset with individuals, no matter who they were. I started focusing more on what was happening in the spiritual realm rather than what was happening in the physical realm. To think that I could also be used by satan was disconcerting. I would have to make sure that never happened. But I also realized that I could not do that in my power alone. I needed the help of the Spirit. I needed Him to help me walk in and with Him daily so that I would not become a vessel for satan's activities. I knew this was easier said than done but we can only accomplish this when we ask the Spirit to help us. This rhema word that the Holy Spirit gave to me was powerful and life changing. The Holy Spirit Guides and Protects Us As We Develop The Habit Of Listening To Him

As I mentioned above, to practice listening to the Holy Spirit we must cultivate an atmosphere of silence and stillness. Try not to disobey His voice when He speaks to us. He will tell us things we may not want to hear, such as moments when we are with friends, and we are anxious to share a juicy bit of gossip. He prompts us not to share that information. Sometimes He will even tell us the reasons why we should not share that information. I believe if we keep ignoring the voice, after a time the voice will stop teaching us, guiding us, giving us wisdom and will stop protecting us. Likewise, if the Holy Spirit knows that we are obedient, He will continue to speak to us and give us all the above benefits. As you will see from the rest of my story below, some of these benefits are lifesaving. We should not live without His daily guidance., wisdom, and protection. That is why it is so important to listen and obey His voice. Some of the instances that I am about to recall were moments when I was in great danger and the Holy Spirit spoke to me. I honestly believe that the practice of listening to Him over the years and obeying His voice saved y life when I was in danger. I do not believe I would have discerned or obeyed His voice had I not practiced the discipline of hearing and obeying Him.

5. The Spirit Guides And Protects Us With His Strong Promptings

I have had a lot of encounters with the Holy Spirit, some great and some small. Although I decided to write about the ones that I think were jaw dropping, some of the simple ones were just as amazing and taught me so much about how the Holy Spirit hears us each time we pray and comes to our aid. Now I am sure some of you readers can relate to this example. You are late for an appointment. You cannot find your car keys. You only have two minutes to find them. You are searching and it is hopeless. This happened to me so many times. Then I remembered that I did not pray and ask the Spirit to help me find them or whatever it was that I was searching for. So, after being frustrated I would say "Holy Spirit I did it again, here I am wasting time looking and not praying and asking for your help." As soon as I prayed, like instantly after I prayed, I would be led to look in places I had not been looking and I would usually readily find them, And I usually would find found them within the two minutes or less. Multiply that by 10 times or more and that was how often it has happened to me. Each time I was amazed at how the Spirit always helps me as soon as I prayed This increases my faith tremendously as it has happened to me so many times!

Now I am getting excited because I am about to tell you about three significant encounters that I had with the Holy Spirit. First, I would like to thank Dean for allowing me to share these moments with you and I pray that after you read about these encounters you will embrace the Spirit even more. For those of you who wonders if He is for real, I pray that these encounters will confirm in your heart and in your spirit that He is the real deal. I hope it will also confirm how much He loves you and wants the best for you every day. He watches over you like a hawk.

He sometimes reminds me of a good bodyguard. You have seen them on TV. While everyone is enjoying watching the President walk through the crowd, the bodyguards 'eyes are all over the people, intensely watching everyone and everything so that no harm comes to the President. That is a simplified example, as the Holy Spirit does so much more than that for us in realtime!

Holy Spirit Encounter No. 1: Walking Through My Neighborhood

I live in a residential neighborhood in Tampa, Florida. It is mostly peaceful and quiet. I try to keep fit by walking in the evenings. And I say "try" because I struggle to keep motivated, and I do not like walking when it is dark. This was the fall season when the sun sets early, and I was walking at about 7:00 pm and already dark. A large cream-colored American car drove past me. It stopped about 1000 feet from me on the opposite side of the road, but I did not think anything of it as it was not exhibiting anything unusual. I was walking fast getting closer to the car. I heard a voice speaking to me. It was not an audible voice – it was a strong prompting voice that I heard in my spirit saying, "do not pass that car.". It was difficult to obey because I tend not to be afraid of anyone or anything. The elementary school that I had attended had a lot of bullies. One of the best things that school did for me was make me strong and fearless. I did not obey the voice and I kept walking, getting closer to the car. When I did not obey, the voice got louder, and shouted "DO NOT PASS THAT CAR!" I knew right away that I needed to obey this voice, so I started to jog in the opposite direction. The car started to spin around extremely fast but because of its size it had to reverse to make the turn. While the car was trying to turn around, I started running for my life. I only had seconds to think - If I ran through one of the yards, it would take me to my house. The problem was that those houses that would take me home were several houses down the street, and I could not get to them fast enough. It was too risky, so for some reason I ran across the street and into the yard on the other side.

I could hear the wheels of the car trying to make the turn. I knocked forcefully on the door thinking that that person would let me in. The lady came to the door and peered thorough the window in the door. It took me seconds to realize that she was not going to let me in. Well, da! Who would let a stranger in their house? I was panic stricken! I knew that the car would be there in seconds. I turned to see if the car was at the end of the driveway, and I then realized that there was a solid wall behind and to the side that could hide me. The lady was still peering though the window in the door. I could tell that even though she would not let me in, I believed that she wanted to help me. I put my fingers to my ears signaling to call the police. She came back to the window and started dialing as the car drove up. I could see the front of the car, but they could not see me phone in her hand and she was looking directly at them. I suspect they thought I was in the house with the lady, that she was calling the police so they did not tarry, and rapidly drove off. After they departed, I hurried off for home as the lady never did offer for me to come in. Only the Spirit knows what He avoided for me if I had not obeyed. As I was thinking about including this incident in this testimony, I thought about something else. What if that house that I ran to happened to be the only house on the street with a wall in front to protect me? I decided to drive over to see, and sure enough, no other home on that street had such a wall. Thank you, again, Holy Spirit!

This experience still upsets me every time I recall it.

Holy Spirit Encounter No. 2: Driving to The Airport

A few years ago, my daughter was flying in from Fort Lauderdale to visit me. I was very excited because she was bringing my one-year-old grandchild. I was running late so I took a short cut through a neighborhood. The road was very dark and that was the first time I traveled it at night. I remember saying to myself that this would be the last time I would travel here at night as there were no streetlights. As I was thinking this, a car came on the opposite side of the road with its full beam on. This was a long road and with the bright lights from this car, I could see very little directly in front of me.

I decided to reduce my speed to about 20 miles an hour. I then heard a voice prompting me, just like the voice I heard on my walk – it clearly said "stop". Again, I questioned it and did not obey. My question was, why should I stop. I am driving in my lane nowhere close to the shoulder of the road. This road had no sidewalk and over the years I could not recall seeing anyone walking on it. While I was questioning why I should stop in the middle of the road, I started driving even more slowly and the car with the full beam was just about to pass me. Visibility was at its worse. I could see nothing. I reduced my speed to about 10 miles per hour. The voice shouted at me to "STOP!". I immediately slammed on my brakes and stopped!

The car with the full beam passed and suddenly I could see everything clearly. What I saw immediately in front of the car shocked me! I saw an inebriated couple in the middle of my lane about 10 feet from my front bumper. They were both laughing and swaying from left to right. If I had not obeyed the voice I would have run over them and possibly killed them. I immediately became a nervous wreck. When I thought of what could have happened, I started to shake uncontrollably. I pulled the car over to the side of the road and stopped. They looked back at my car and continued laughing and swaying down the middle of the road oblivious to what could have happened to them. For a few moments, I prayed thankfulness to the Holy Spirit for His guidance and protection over me and over that couple. As I drove to the airport, I was nervous and shaken. I kept pondering on the goodness of the Holy Spirit and thanking and praising Him for His protection.

Holy Spirit Encounter No. 3: My Olive Oil and Garlic concoction

I have always enjoyed steamed cabbage. I started loving it more when I decided to cut rice and mashed potatoes from my diet and add cabbage. I went to the store and bought a bottle of olive oil with garlic and red peppers. I added this to my steamed cabbage, and it was delicious. When I ran out of the olive oil, I went back to the store and found that they were sold out and they had no idea when they would be getting more. I was disappointed but not for long as I decided to make my own concoction. I went back to the store and bought some extra virgin olive oil and a bag of fresh garlic. I had garlic in my freezer, but I wanted fresh garlic. I also wanted to start adding kale to my smoothie, so I also bought kale.

When I got home, I put the olive oil, garlic and the kale on the kitchen counter. I was getting ready to make my own concoction, but I wanted to freeze the kale first and get that out of the way. I went on my computer and typed into Google "how to freeze kale." As I finished typing, a pop-up box came at me. I'm sure that you are familiar with these annoying boxes that advertise things that you do not want. This box was not advertising anything however and I questioned why would I type in "how to freeze kale" and get a pop-up box on "how to freeze garlic?" It did not make sense. I was annoyed as I had been freezing garlic for years and that was the last thing I needed to know. I was about to close the pop-up by clicking on the little red box, when I heard a voice say, "do not close the box." As usual, I questioned the voice and I said to myself "I do not need to read an article on how to freeze garlic. I already know and I have lots of frozen garlic in my freezer." As I was about to close the box, the voice was very firm saying, "DO NOT CLOSE THE BOX, READ IT!" Because of my experiences over the years with this firm voice, I heeded it as I was seconds away from closing the box. I reluctantly clicked on the article and started to read it. In short, the article said do not immerse garlic cloves in olive oil. That was exactly what I was about to do in a few minutes! The article went on to state that this garlic-induced olive oil creates an anaerobic environment that causes "botulism." The lack of oxygen created the dangerous growth of botulism spores and neither refrigeration nor freezing would stop the growth of these spores. I continued reading the article found that what was even more alarming was that after ingesting the olive oil and garlic, no stomach aches and no vomiting, and you could be dead within three days after ingesting it. It was a silent killer! OMGod! I started shaking like I shook after that car incident as I realized how close I came to killing myself and my husband. I had no intention of refrigerating my concoction after that! The Holy Spirit had only seconds to stop me from closing that "pop-up box". I thank the Holy Spirit that He prompted me to hear Him and to obey His voice immediately. I find His protection so amazing – so beyond words.

These are incidents that I can recall, and I often reflect on incidents that He has probably saved me from that I am not even aware of. All I can do is thank Him and praise Him for His awesome presence in my life!

Whether you have been walking with the Holy Spirit, just getting to know Him or you are not sure who He is, my prayer is that you will seek Him. Ask Him questions about Himself and enjoy the journey with Him. He is Jesus' representative on earth. Jesus told us that when He leaves to go to His Father in Heaven, He would send us the Holy Spirit as our Counselor and our Comforter, and that is what Jesus has done. The Holy Spirit lives in us, guides us, directs us, empowers us, gives us wisdom, prays for us, protects us and so much more. He covets a close relationship with you but He will not force you into it. He will wait for you to make that decision. If you have never made that decision, invite Him into your heart and life today, and you will be blessed beyond your greatest expectations

CHAPTER 21
A MOVIE OF YOUR LIFE

One of the best ways of visualizing your relationship with the Trinity is to imagine that you come to a theater, and the movie is a documentary of your life. The movie has a Producer (Heavenly Father) who knows your story line in every detail from the beginning to the end of your life. He has defined the ending, and He knows the impact that He wants to leave with those who have come to know you. He knows the legacy that He wants you to leave when your life on earth is over.

Next, every movie has a Director (our Lord Jesus) who takes the story and makes it come alive on the screen. He knows your story in detail from before you were born to the present day and has developed the story line, including the ending, along with the Producer.

The third important person that has produced your true-life story is the Scriptwriter. He (the Holy Spirit) works out all the details necessary to make this storyline complete in coordination with the Producer and Director. He works directly with you in every detail throughout your life. Obviously, He also knows your life from beginning to the end, with the desired results defined by the Producer and Director. Important to them also is the resulting impact on the viewers of your movie - your family, friends and others that have come to know you throughout your life.

As it is in all movies, these three persons are *invisible* to you and the viewers of your movie. They work behind the scenes in every detail of your story and have the ability to make your movie complete and successful in the Producer's eyes. This same Producer will be orchestrating the lives of others who are touched by your life as well, many of whom you may never know.

And now for the most important participant in this movie - you. When the movie comes to the present day, *you* become the main character of the movie. The question is, what kind of person will you play out to the end of your life? Will you study what the Producer and Director would like you to be, following the script faithfully? Or, will you continue to want to conduct your role your way and on your terms? Will you continue to ignore them and their advice, or will you trust them and follow what they want you to do, scene by scene. A successful actor devotes his time to analyzing the main character in detail, learns the script and faithfully follows and portrays what he is directed to do. In this way the movie will have the greatest success with the greatest impact on the viewers, and it will display your best legacy.

Each challenge that you will be facing in your remaining days can also be looked at the same way. Will you be faithful to the plan that the Producer, Director and Scriptwriter have already developed that is far better than any plan that you could develop, or will you continue to do it your way and ignore them. You need to realize that you don't know what tomorrow will bring, and they know every detail of your remaining days. Will you trust them totally, partially or not at all. As a believer you know that your way could not possibly be as good as theirs. You must be aware that the remaining life you live from this very moment on will be the consequences of your willingness to trust and obey, or not.

"...let us run with endurance the race that is set before us, fixing our eyes on Jesus the author and perfecter of faith..." (Hebrews 12:1-2)

Now to him who is able to do immeasurably more than all we ask or imagine according to His power that is at work within us, to Him be glory in the church and in Christ Jesus throughout all generations, for ever and ever. Amen

Ephesians 4:20-21

There may be many, many people that you may yet be impacting in your life to come. Some of them may owe their life to you physically as a result of the help you may be offering them during their time of need. If you have empathy for others, there may be some that may be impacted by what you say to them, what you do to help them in their struggles, or how you live your life as an example to them. You may have talents that, if channeled for worthwhile efforts, may encourage others to make their own lives more meaningful. If you seek a stronger relationship with our Lord, He may lead you into an inspired career for the remainder of your life that is beyond your wildest imagine. He may bring someone into your life that may stimulate your creative life at the time you had about lost hope for the future. He may bring someone into your life when you have a desperate need for help. He may restore relationships that have otherwise been lost. He may bring renewed adventure back into your spirit that you may have never expected to be restored. He may bring innovation and stimulated ideas when you had lost confidence in yourself. The Lord has a unique plan for you, each day for the rest of your life – do you want to learn to live it to its fullest? If so, passionately seek first the living Lord Jesus through the Holy Spirit, and you can expect to be amazed at what your future could be! The Trinity will *never* force you to do something. The Lord is a counselor, encourager, helper and friend, but you must devote yourself to do your part and not wait for Him to do it all for you.

What a friend we have in Jesus –
All our sins and grief to bear!
What a privilege to carry\
Everything to God in prayer!
O what peace we often forfeit,
O what needless pain we bear,
All because we do not carry
Everything to God in prayer!

Have we trials and temptations?
Is there trouble anywhere?
We should never be discouraged,
Take it to the Lord in prayer.

Can we find a friend so faithful
Who will all our sorrows share?
Jesus knows our every weakness,
Take it to the Lord in prayer.

Are we weak and heavy-laden,
Cumbered with a load of care?
Precious Savior, still our refuge –
Take it to the Lord in prayer;

Do thy friends despise, forsake thee?
Take it to the Lord in prayer;
In His arms He'll take and shield thee,
Thou wilt find a solace there.

Text by Joseph M. Scriven

CHAPTER 22

CONCLUDING THOUGHTS TO PONDER

Today the greatest lack, prevalent throughout most of Christendom, is the awareness of the power of the Holy Spirit in every detail of life. To prove this point, I ask you to consider the billions of dollars that have been spent on Christian activities throughout the world during the last generation (let's say 50 years) and yet what effect has there been in society? Has the standard of worthiness been advanced? Are the churches fuller and less worldly? Are the members more Christ-like in their daily life? If you asked them individually, including the pastors, to give you a clear example of where the Holy Spirit has been evident in their life during the past week, who could give you a testimony? Is there more godliness in the homes of Christians? Are children more respectable and obedient? Has the standard of honesty and integrity been raised in our society? Are we willing to take God up on His promises for financial security in the future or are we focused on the need for retirement programs for our assurances? Are American Christians satisfied with their meager contributions or even satisfied with their tithing obligation considering that all the rest is theirs to spend on their own creature comforts, while the needs of others all around them go unheeded? Are we focused on being "self-sufficient", comfortable in every way so that we don't have any genuine needs in the future when we would need to seek the Lord's help? How much time is spent in our daily life consciously aware that we are in the presence of the Living Lord?

We can decide what to do to build our faith and trust in our relationship with the Trinity, but we must first seek the presence and power of the Holy Spirit to guide and direct our path towards our Christian future. However, appealing to His presence is one thing but we must *await for His guidance and inspiration!* Remember, the Holy Spirit is with us *at all times* - be aware of His presence and talk to Him as a friend who is ever present as we live and move and have our being! He is omnipresent (everywhere), omniscient (knowing everything), and omnipotent (having unlimited power).

Jesus was conceived by the Holy Spirit (Matthew 1:18). Jesus was baptized with the Holy Spirit (Matthew 3:16) Jesus was led by the Holy Spirit (Matthew 4:1 and Luke 4:1). The Holy Spirit leads men. (Acts 13:4). The Holy Spirit provides inspiration to develop spiritual gifts. (1 Corinthians 12:1 thru 11).

When you ask the Lord to come into your life and believe in His resurrection, His acceptance guarantees your "ticket" to salvation and forever in heaven. From there the Holy Spirit, under the direction of Jesus, works with you and slowly "cleans you out". If you enthusiastically accept the Holy

Spirit working with you, He will do amazing things with you. His desire is not to just do good things for you and help you develop your fruits of the Spirit, but also to guide you to a personal ministry to help others find their relationship with the Lord.

If by now you have digested this book and appreciate the importance of having the Holy Spirit help you with your struggles in life, I would like to encourage you to embrace the following suggestions. If your daily life is full of challenges and demands where you feel that your life is out of control, I would suggest that you begin with a blank sheet of writing paper. Itemize those issues that are consuming your time and stealing your mental freedom. Use an overall statement for each of them like you are presenting them to the Lord, bearing in mind that He already knows more about then than you do. Remember that the Holy Spirit wants to help you to find the answers and solutions, not fixing the situation for you. As an example, if you have an issue with your car, don't expect that He is going to miraculously fix it, but He will give you guidance in your search for the best solution. Include in your list of issues everything such that if they were all resolved, you would be free of worry and anxiety.

The next most important thing is to develop a consistent routine of always going on your knees in prayer before you get into bed. Consider this a time to talk to Him in prayer, conversing with Him as your best friend. Take this list of issues and present them in the simplified form that you have written them out. After presenting them to Him, place the list on a dresser or nearby table, and go to bed. *Cast them out of your mind – don't dwell on them!* Thank Him then, knowing that He is more than willing to accept being responsible for resolving each of them in His time and in His way, and ask Him to exchange them for His peace that is beyond all understanding. Knowing that He takes on the overall responsibility for resolution, go to sleep with a sense of relief that He promises to work with you and that He will not forget. Ask Him also for a good, solid night's sleep that you can use as a clear indication that He has heard you. In the morning, train your mind to say hello to Him as the first thought, thank Him for the good night's sleep, and ask Him to guide and direct you through all of the priorities that He has for you that day. If you wake up before it is time to get up, talk to Him about the things that you are thankful for before you go to Him with your concerns. Be enthusiastic about knowing that He has all of your cares in his hand and He will lead you through all of the issues that you are facing that day. Avoid reviewing those concerns that you don't need to have an answer for that day - only take one day at a time. In the coming days seek the clues of His work in progress towards resolution on those issues yet to be resolved. As you go through the day, talk to Him when you can, while driving, when details of an issue comes up mentally, consult Him, be calm and patient, and when a decision is needed consult Him as the moment allows. If things are not going easy, it is no surprise to Him and by asking Him, He will help you through it and you will learn from it.

By making the above approach to life's daily issues, you will find far more peace of mind, a better night's sleep, better solutions will evolve, and your life will have less stress and more joy. What you will come to realize is that The Holy Spirit has been waiting all of your life for you to wake up to the reality that He is the real deal, and wants you to ask for His involvement in your life. He will not force Himself on you, and He is delighted when you want a relationship! If you take time to reflect on your past, you will find plenty of evidence that He has been providing blessings all along, and He knows you personally, by name. However, nothing but the mighty power of the Holy Spirit can turn or lead your heart in a direction away from the love of the things of this world.

And now, this is His calling to you:

Will you come and follow Me if I but call your name?
Will you go where you don't know and never be the same?
Will you let My love be shown, will you let My name be known,
Will you let My life be grown in you and you in Me?

Will you love the "you" you hide if I but call your name?
Will you quell the fear inside and never be the same?
Will you use the faith you've found to reshape the world around
Through My sight and touch and sound in you and you in Me?

Your answer?

Let me turn and follow You and never be the same.
In Your company I'll go, where Your love and footsteps show,
Thus, I'll move and live and grow, in you and you in Me.

John L. Bell

CHAPTER 23
PROCLAMATION

As I am attempting to finish this manuscript, I am inspired to emphasize the need for all of us to ponder what is wrong with our world.

With the virus and other significant events this last year or so, we all sense that something is happening to alter what we have considered as "normal". I feel a calling to point out to everyone who will read this book with a serious consideration, I believe that the Lord is actively moving to confront the evil that we all are experiencing. Our Creator could not be pleased with the condition of mankind. From a God's-eye prospective, I believe that there is no place in the world that pleases Him – not even the United States that is the last bastion of freedom. The Old Testament is filled with examples of when a society has drifted away significantly from God's dictates, becoming unworthy of His blessings, He eventually takes revenge for the purpose of proving that He is still in control of all details! Not only has our entire society actively moved away from His principles, even most Christian brothers and sisters are not understanding and professing an understanding of life fully devoted to embracing a vital part of the Trinity – the Holy Spirit.

All peoples throughout the world are experiencing a serious breakdown of the freedoms and values in our societies. Abortion is the law of the land, even up to birth. Democracy is being seriously threatened as socialism is being actively promoted. Freedom of the press has been undermined by a monopoly of big-money influence in news manipulation, doing everything possible to suppress the truth. Labor unions have become so powerful in the major cities throughout the country that many of them are being governed by leadership allowing the quality of living to be severely eroded. Our healthcare industry is one of the largest businesses in the country with the pharmaceutical companies supporting and actually preventing medical doctors from using all-natural therapies unless approved ty the Food and Drug Administration that is heavily influenced by the greed of the American Medical Association.

Using the Covid-19 virus as an excuse, nearly every aspect of our society is being dictated to by our government including schools, churches, restaurants, beauty shops, small businesses and entertainment establishments. Every aspect of our society is seriously impacted by the legal profession that cultivates lawsuits for even frivolous issues especially against large corporations that find it less costly to give in to minor or false accusations than to fight them. This drives the cost of everything much higher than it should be, and it affects us all greatly. Couples are now marrying less and living together as often as not. Credit is sky high as we buy more and more things to satisfy our pleasurers and desires, much more than just our needs and helping the less fortunate.

Our homes are no longer 1200 to 1500 square feet with eight-foot ceilings and are now more like 2500 to 4000 square feet with 10 and 12 foot ceilings. Two cars are in nearly every driveway, and often more. Most homes have at least two TV's and it is common to have a large one in the family room, one in the kitchen and one in each bedroom. Often everyone in the family has their own smartphone – even young children. It is not uncommon for a college graduate to have accumulated over $100,000 in debt.

All of this abundance is very common for a significant percentage of our population in the United States and yet our homeless population is alarmingly high. Many are living in tents, under overpasses, or in woodlands. Much of this is happening while at the same time jobs are plentiful, as many are willing to live on welfare alone. Exorbitant taxes and fees are sucking people's incomes, driving many out of cities and states while those who remain have to carry even higher burden of taxation. In some areas of our country retired people end up having to sell their home because of unaffordable taxes and fees.

What is wrong with this scenario – in the land of the free and the home of the brave? In the land where dreams and hard work have always paid off with great rewards? Especially since the virus, government control has affected nearly all aspects of our life, about the only real agreement among everyone is that what we use to consider as "normal" no longer is or will probably ever be the same. There is not one person in the world that has not been affected by significant changes of some kind in recent times. No wonder we all sense that God is about to do something dramatic.

It is commonly understood, however, that there also has been much positive changes in many areas caused by the virus. As an example, air pollution has been dramatically reduced – worldwide. Before the virus, the most polluted city in the world was New Delhi, India with whatever scale of measurement is used, the pollution index averaged over 200 – extremely unhealthy, both inside and outside of the home. Three months into the virus with resultant lockdowns, business closures and associated shutdown of many businesses, the pollution average in New Delhi dropped to 10 to 15, and occasionally down to a seven. Families all over the world have been forced to eat meals together instead of individually catch their own meals, usually eating out in restaurants and fast-food places. It is common to see families now walking bicycling or hiking together instead of young babies being raised in daycare centers, it is much more often they are raised by their mothers or other family members. Homeschooling is much more common now which is considered a better education than low-quality public schools that are teaching subjects that are in conflict with the Bible. Single young people are commonly living with their parents as well as recently married couples that can have a positive effect if done properly.

It is also true that there are significant downsides that have resulted from the virus. Unemployment has significantly increased with resultant poverty levels on the rise. Those marriages that were in trouble before the virus often are negatively impacted. Despair and discouragement is commonplace, with the suicide rate on a significant rise. Financial hardship is very often the case, resulting in higher stress levels. Where relationships were struggling in the past, the current living conditions often exacerbate the dissentions.

Christian believers are still firmly convinced that God is still in control, and soon will be causing a significant impact of some kind on our society and in the world. The Old Testament is very clear that when kings and kingdoms drift away from His worthiness, eventually He takes drastic action. It seems clearly evident that the entire world now is adrift away from His dictates.

In the third chapter of the book of Revelations 3:14, John was directed by, "... the Amen, the faithful and true witness, the ruler of God's creation (Jesus), John was directed to write, "I know your deeds, that you are neither cold nor hot. I wish you were either one! So, because you are lukewarm – neither hot nor cold – I am about to spit you out of my mouth. You say, "I am rich, I have acquired wealth and do not need a thing." But you do not realize that you are wrenched, pitiful, poor, blind and naked."

It is time to analyze where we are individually in our spiritual fervor (defined as intense and passionate feeling), hot, cold or lukewarm. Where is spiritual fervor in your church – in Christianity in America – in Christianity throughout the world? At this time in history, we should be convicted to be serious about developing a passionate relationship with our Lord Jesus, through our own personal Holy Spirit!

In Matthew 7:21, Jesus says that not everyone who calls me Lord will enter the kingdom of heaven, but only he who does the will of my Father. Have you developed a personal relationship with the Lord and from that determined the plans that He has for you personally? We were created to have a personal relationship – He doesn't need our money or our deeds – He only wants our sincere love and appreciation for all that He has already faithfully provided to us even though we didn't deserve it or recognized it. After we come to Him for a relationship, if we let Him, He will then guide us to the deeds, plans and attitudes that He wants for us – not what we "think" would please Him. Only He knows your "tomorrow". Will you let Him work with you to define it or will you continue to try to control your future? A saying worthy to dwell on is, "Stop the illusion that you are in control of your future." It is definitely an illusion, as we can only guess what tomorrow will bring - but He knows!

Carry on my dear reader and come to realize that a new day full of love, joy and hope is awaiting you despite the struggles of living in this broken world.